Cambodia

Cambodia

BY SARA LOUISE KRAS

Enchantment of the World
Second Series

Children's Press®

A Division of Scholastic Inc.

NEW YORK TORONTO LONDON AUCKLAND SYDNEY
MEXICO CITY NEW DELHI HONG KONG
DANBURY, CONNECTICUT

Frontispiece: A temple at Angkor

Consultant: Kheang Un, Political Science Department, Northern Illinois University,
            Dekalb, Illinois

Please note: *All statistics are as up-to-date as possible at the time of publication.*

Book production by Herman Adler Design

Library of Congress Cataloging-in-Publication Data

Kras, Sara Louise.
  Cambodia / by Sara Louise Kras. — 1st ed.
     p. cm. — (Enchantment of the world. Second series)
  Includes bibliographical references and index.
  ISBN 0-516-23679-2
  1. Cambodia—Juvenile literature. I. Title. II. Series.
  DS554.3.K73 2005
  959.6—dc22   2004026192

Cambodia

Contents

Cover photo:
A Khmer wearing
a krama

Angkor Wat

An Ancient Kingdom in a Modern World

HUGE STONE TEMPLES COVERED WITH GOLD SHIMMER in the jungle. Nearby is a grand palace. Here comes a royal parade!

The parade begins with troops of horsemen. Next come musicians pounding on drums and blowing on conch shells and flutes. They are followed by beautiful girls with flowers flowing from their hair. The girls dance to the music while holding candles. Behind them are elephants carrying noblemen and government ministers. They sit under bright red umbrellas that sway with each step. And then, at the end of the parade, comes the king. He is standing straight up on an elephant's back, holding a shiny sacred sword high in the air.

Cambodia was once home to a grand kingdom called Angkor. The splendid palaces and temples of Angkor were built between the ninth and the fourteenth centuries. The palaces were made of wood.

Today, these palaces are gone. But the grand stone temples remain. The temple walls are covered with huge numbers of carvings. These carvings provide a glimpse

Opposite: **Angkor temple**

Carvings on the walls of ancient temples depict life in the Angkor kingdom.

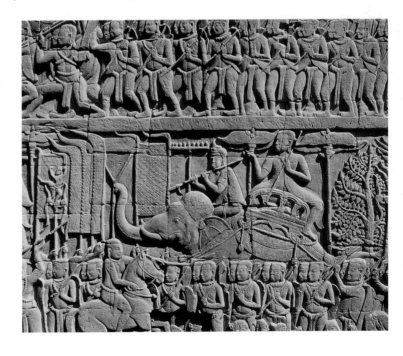

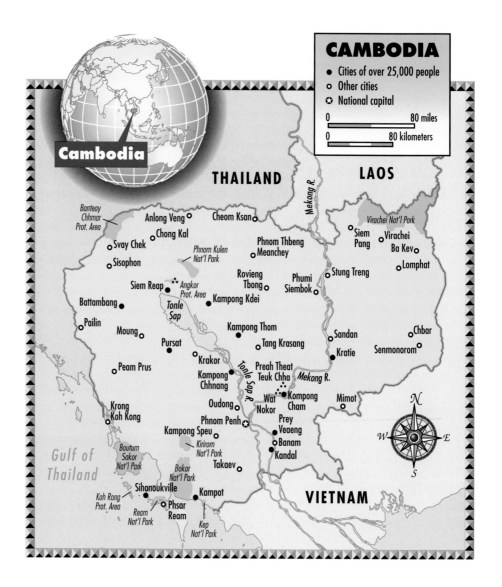

into life in the Angkor kingdom. The carvings show the ancient Cambodian people casting fishing nets out into the Tonle Sap, Cambodia's largest lake. They show people walking next to oxcarts weighed down with fish and rice. Carvings depict women spinning cloth and men making bricks. These pictures were carved eight hundred to nine hundred years ago. Yet similar scenes take place in Cambodia today.

Even now in the early morning, a boy living near the Tonle Sap helps his father cast nets into the water. While he waits for the nets to fill up with fish, the boy jumps in the water to splash and play with his friends.

During the dry season, an oxcart is piled high with harvested rice. A farmer steers the oxen to the village. Women prepare the rice. First, they pound it with poles to loosen the husks. Then the rice is placed in a flat bamboo tray and shaken back and forth and tossed in the air to separate it from the straw and husks.

Today, soft silk is harvested from silkworms. Girls are taught to weave the silk into pink, purple, and turquoise fabrics.

A merchant shows off silk cloth at a market in Phnom Penh.

In the ancient kingdom of Angkor, dancers performed only for the king. Today, locals and tourists alike watch Cambodian dancers at theaters and hotels. These dancers move their hands and feet in graceful, flowing movements. Their heads are crowned with tall, golden headdresses. Gold bracelets, necklaces, and anklets adorn their poised bodies.

Just as in ancient times, Cambodians still ride on elephants. Tourists to Cambodia can ride these lumbering creatures to visit temples of the Angkor kingdom.

Visitors can ride an elephant taxi at Angkor Wat.

After many years of war and foreign occupation, modern Cambodia again has a king. The king's palace is elaborately decorated in white and gold. The country is called a constitutional monarchy. This is a more modern view toward kingship, where the king reigns but elected officials govern.

Signs of modern life are everywhere in Cambodia. Motorcycles whiz by on the streets of the capital city of Phnom Penh. Internet cafés buzz with activity. Airplanes come and go. Speedboats zip up and down the Mekong River.

Yet even as Cambodia quickly moves into the modern world, it still maintains its ancient traditions of elephants, dancers, and kings.

Motorcycles are a popular way of getting around in Cambodia.

An Ancient Kingdom in a Modern World **13**

The Land
of Water

CAMBODIA IS A COUNTRY DRIVEN BY THE EBB AND FLOW of water from the Mekong River and the Tonle Sap lake. It is a country of lush vegetation, with rice paddies, giant strangler fig trees, banyan trees, and lily pads.

Cambodia is shaped like a big rice bowl. It is located on the Indochina peninsula in Southeast Asia. This peninsula gets its name from its location between India and China. Cambodia lies along the Gulf of Thailand. It is wedged between Thailand and Laos to the north and northwest and Vietnam to the east and southeast.

Cambodia is about the size of Missouri. In its center are lowland plains. Mountain chains rise to the east, west, and north of these plains.

Opposite: **Boating on the Tonle Sap lake**

Western Cambodia borders the Gulf of Thailand.

The Mekong River runs through the middle of the country, splitting it in two. The Mekong is the longest river in Southeast Asia. It is also the tenth-longest river in the world.

Many Cambodians survive by fishing in the Mekong River.

The Mekong flows out of the Himalaya Mountains of Tibet and runs for about 2,600 miles (4,200 kilometers). It crosses China and creates most of the border between Laos and Thailand before flowing into Cambodia.

Within Cambodia, the Mekong River runs for 315 miles (507 km). At Phnom Penh, the Tonle Sap River—which spills from the Tonle Sap lake—joins the Mekong. The water then divides into two rivers, the Mekong and Bassac rivers, which flow south into Vietnam. The Mekong ends its long journey in southern Vietnam, where it flows into the South China Sea.

The Mekong is home to more than 1,500 species of freshwater fish, one of Cambodia's main food items. Only the Amazon River in South America and the Congo River in Africa have a greater variety of fish.

Cambodia's Geographic Features

Highest Point: Phnum Aoral, 5,948 feet (1,813 m) above sea level

Lowest Point: Sea level along the Gulf of Thailand

Longest River: Mekong River, 315 miles (507 km) within Cambodia

Largest Lake: Tonle Sap, for six months each year, about 4,020 square miles (10,400 sq km)

Longest Shared Border: 763 miles (1,228 km), with Vietnam

Highest Average Temperature: 85°F (29.5°C) in April

Lowest Average Temperature: 78°F (25.6°C) in January

Greatest Precipitation: 200 inches (508 cm) in the mountains along the southwest coast

Greatest Distance North to South: 280 miles (451 km)

Greatest Distance East to West: 350 miles (563 km)

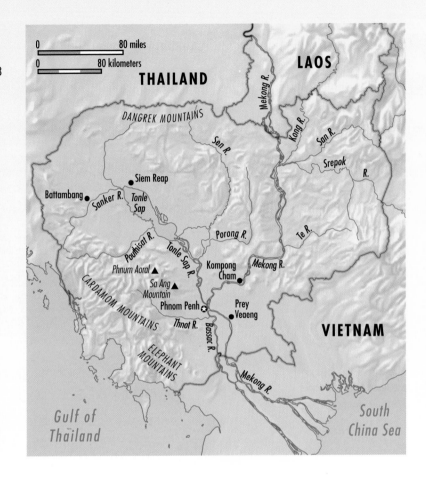

The Great Lake

Tonle Sap means "great lake." In fact, the Tonle Sap is the largest freshwater lake in Southeast Asia. The huge body of water stretches through the west-central part of Cambodia. The lake drains at its southeast point into the Tonle Sap River, which flows into the Mekong.

Some families along the Tonle Sap live in floating houses.

When the rainy season begins in late May or early June, the Mekong River starts to swell. The Mekong grows in size both from rainfall and from the melting snow in Tibet, where the river begins. The high waters of the Mekong cause the Tonle Sap River to reverse its flow up into the lake. Because of this, the Tonle Sap lake expands in size. It grows from 1,000 square miles to 4,020 square miles (2,600 sq km to 10,400 sq km). The lake is four times larger during the rainy season than during the dry season!

Some families live in huts that can be taken apart and moved as the lake's shoreline shifts. The Tonle Sap is also home to many floating villages. People live in houses that float on bamboo. These floating houses often have fish pens underneath, where fish are fattened up before they are eaten.

Many kinds of fish live in the Tonle Sap. The largest is the giant Mekong catfish. This fish can reach lengths of almost 10 feet (3 meters) and weigh more than 600 pounds (270 kilograms).

The Tonle Sap is thick with fish and other aquatic life. This makes fishing very easy. Fishing is easiest when the waters recede. This can happen with incredible speed. It can happen so fast that the fish cannot keep up with the water. Sometimes fishermen simply pick the fish off the tree branches they had cut and placed underwater only a short time before.

The elephant fish has adapted to this problem of quickly receding waters. It can survive out of the water in the wet mud for several hours. This gives it time to flap and flip its way back to the water.

A man empties his fish trap on the Tonle Sap.

Disastrous Floods

The Mekong River and the Tonle Sap can sometimes swell way beyond even their normal rainy season size. This can result in disastrous flooding.

A flood in July 2000 injured fifty-one people and killed fifteen. The flood wreaked havoc in Phnom Penh, the capital city, which lies along the banks of the Mekong River. A teenage boy drowned in front of the Royal Palace. On the Tonle Sap, villagers were trapped in houses built on stilts. Rescue workers arrived in boats to save them.

In September 2001, disastrous flooding again hit Cambodia. Fifty-six people died and 900,000 were left homeless. They had to stay in schools and temples on higher ground until the waters receded.

When the Tonle Sap's waters recede, they leave behind mud filled with nutrients. This mud makes for very fertile farmland. Local farmers take advantage of this, growing deep-water rice that is unique to this area. The Mekong's cycle of flooding and receding is vital for farmers, who grow rice and vegetables along its riverbanks.

Central Lowlands and Coast

Cambodia's central lowlands are very flat and are covered with rice fields, farmland, and grasslands. These fertile plains, which cover about one-third of the country, are where most of the people live. The temperature of the lowlands is quite warm and nearly constant at around 85°F (29°C).

Cambodia's coast along the Gulf of Thailand is 220 miles (354 km) long. The sea is filled with fish. White sandy beaches and uninhabited islands are common along the coast.

A fairly new city called Sihanoukville lies along the coast. This city was founded in 1955, after Cambodia became independent from France. It was established as Cambodia's main

Sihanoukville

Sihanoukville was named after King Norodom Sihanouk, who was king when the city was founded.

ocean port. Prior to this, all goods were brought in via the Mekong River through Vietnam, another French colony.

Ko Nang Yuan is one of the many islands off the coast of Cambodia.

Mountain Ranges

Surrounding the central plains are the Cardamom, Elephant, and Dangrek mountains. The Cardamom Mountains are located in southwestern Cambodia. They are named after cardamom spice, which grows in Southeast Asia. The highest point in Cambodia, Phnum Aoral, is in the Cardamom Mountains.

These mountains have remained fairly isolated over the years because of poor roads and because the region was dangerous during Cambodia's violent recent history. Because of the isolation, the Cardamom Mountains are the largest wilderness in mainland Southeast Asia, more than 2.5 million acres

Fewer than five thousand Siamese crocodiles remain in the world. Most are in Cambodia.

(1,012,500 hectares). Today, however, the Cardamom are becoming more accessible.

In the year 2000, a group of British scientists, who were working with the Cambodian Wildlife Protection Office, spent two months exploring the Cardamom range. They were surprised to find hidden treasures. Even today, unusual plants and rare animals survive in the Cardamom. The scientists discovered rare Siamese crocodiles in freshwater marshes. This was a particularly exciting discovery, as it might be the largest remaining population of Siamese crocodiles in the world. On Ghost Mountain, the range's second-highest peak, a scientist found himself surrounded by a herd of rare white elephants.

Conservationists are trying to persuade the Cambodian government to set aside the Cardamom Mountains as a protected area. They need to act quickly because the Cardamom and the animals that live there are in danger. Logging companies are moving higher and higher into the mountains. As they cut down the forests, this unique environment and the animals that live there will disappear.

The Elephant Mountains are located south of the Cardamom and are covered with tropical rain forests. These dense, wet

Cambodia's Protected Areas

Cambodia is filled with ancient ruins and a wide variety of wildlife. The government has created many protected areas to guard these natural treasures.

Cambodia has seven national parks. Riem National Park, which was established in 1993, protects part of the coastline. Twisted mangrove trees rise from the water along its rivers. Coral reefs and seagrass beds thrive underwater. Monkeys, dolphins, and eagles live within the park's boundaries.

Cambodia also has three protected areas. The most famous of these is the Angkor Area. This area is rich in ancient temples.

Cambodia has ten wildlife perches. One of these is Phnum Aoral. This area is home to tigers, elephants, and other endangered species.

Though these areas are officially "protected," Cambodia's park ranger force is small and sometimes ineffective. More rangers are slowly being trained. It is hoped they will be able to protect and maintain these irreplaceable areas.

forests support a wide variety of plants and animals. The Elephant range slopes down into sandy beaches along the coast.

The sheer sandstone cliffs of the Dangrek Mountains create a natural border between Cambodia and Thailand. A road has been built through a pass in these mountains, connecting the two countries. Even so, it is difficult to transport goods along this road.

Climate

Cambodia has a tropical climate. The weather remains hot and humid all year. April is the hottest month, with an average temperature of 85°F (29.5°C). The coldest month, January, still has an average temperature of 78°F (25.6°C).

Lush plant life covers much of Cambodia.

Cambodia has two seasons: the rainy season and the dry season. The seasons are ruled by strong winds called monsoons. The cool, dry, northeastern monsoon blows in from November to April. This wind carries very little rain with it. The southwest monsoon blows in from the Gulf of Thailand and the Indian Ocean from May to October. It brings strong winds and heavy rain. The lowlands can receive up to 55 inches (140 centimeters) of rain during this time.

Cambodia's rainy season runs from May to October.

Looking at Cambodia's Provinces

The largest province in Cambodia is Kompong Cham, which is in southeast Cambodia along the Vietnamese border. Kompong Cham Province has a population of 1,608,914. The province's main town is also called Kompong Cham. Its average temperature in July is 77.9°F (25.5°C) and in January is 78°F (26.0°C).

Kompong Cham Province is filled with temples. Just outside the town of Kompong Cham is Wat Nokor (above). Built in the eleventh century, this temple is a large complex with many alcoves and hidden shrines.

About 24 miles (39 km) outside of town are the ancient ruins of Preah Theat Teuk Chha. These ruins date back a thousand years. The complex once included 551 small temples. Many of these temples were destroyed by the Khmer Rouge, a violent group that held power in the 1970s. Today, only thirty-nine of the temples have been found and identified.

Kandal (below) is the second-largest province in Cambodia, with a population of 1,075,125. This province surrounds Cambodia's capital of Phnom Penh. Sa Ang Mountain is 21 miles (34 km) away from Phnom Penh. A pagoda surrounded by a huge lake rich in fish and flowers sits on its highest peak. Many Cambodians go there during public holidays and traditional festivals.

Siem Reap Province is home to a bustling tourist town also called Siem Reap. It is the gateway to many ancient temples. King Sihanouk's villa is located in the middle of town. It is a small palace, which the king rarely visits. The Siem Reap River divides the town in half. Along its banks is the old French Quarter.

The Wild World

28

CAMBODIA IS FILLED WITH FANTASTIC FORESTS AND RICH lowlands. Many unusual animals and plants make their home there. While some types of wildlife abound in Cambodia, many of the country's most magnificent creatures are in danger of becoming extinct.

Opposite: **Tigers are among Cambodia's most endangered species.**

Creatures Large and Small

Tigers live in the remote forests of the Cardamom Mountains and in other hilly areas. The tiger's coat provides excellent camouflage in the forest. These large creatures are good swimmers but poor tree climbers. Cambodia's wildlife department does not have enough rangers to patrol the areas where the tigers live, so they are often hunted. Today, they are threatened with extinction.

Another endangered cat is the clouded leopard. It has a distinctive coat of orange-brown fur with large irregular markings. Each marking is dark at the edge and lighter in the middle. This clouded fur pattern is what gives the leopard its name. Clouded leopards are found in dense tropical forests. They are excellent climbers.

Clouded leopards live deep in the Cambodian forest.

The Wild World **29**

Cambodia's National Animal

The kouprey, or wild ox, is a symbol of Cambodia's ancient Khmer civilization. In 1964, King Sihanouk declared it Cambodia's national animal. The kouprey is a forest ox that weighs 1,500 to 2,000 pounds (700 to 900 kg). It lives on low, rolling hills and eats mostly grass. The kouprey grazes in open fields during the day. Sometimes it heads into the forest to find shelter from the sun. The forest also offers food when the grasslands are dry and provides protection from predators. Kouprey oxen live in herds of up to twenty, which consist of cows and their calves. During the dry season, bulls might join the herd.

Today, the kouprey is extremely scarce. Some scientists think they may become extinct within ten years.

Other cats in the Cambodian jungle are the leopard cat, the jungle cat, the fishing cat, and the Asian golden cat.

Cambodia is home to several kinds of monkeys, including the macaque and the gibbon. The endangered *douc langur* monkey is found in Cambodia's tropical rain forests. It eats many different types of tree leaves, fruits, and flowers. Douc langur monkeys have become endangered because they have lost much of their forest habitat and they are sometimes hunted for food. Many also died from bombs during the Vietnam War.

Cambodia is also home to bears. Sun bears have short, dark fur. On their

Douc langur monkey

chest is a yellowish white marking that looks like a sun. At 4 feet (1.2 m) long, the sun bear is the world's smallest bear. Sun bears make their home in lowland tropical rain forests and spend most of their time in trees. They often sleep or sunbathe in a nest of branches in the treetops. Another bear found in Cambodia is the endangered Asiatic black bear.

Cambodia's forests are filled with many other types of animals, including tiny deer called the lesser mousedeer, wild pigs, Asian wild dogs, black giant squirrels, Southeast Asian porcupines, and several different types of civets, a catlike creature.

A common domesticated animal in Cambodia is the water buffalo. Some water buffalo can still be found in the wild, but

Sunbears have huge claws that help them climb and get at food.

most are seen working in rice fields or grazing along roadsides. Cambodians use these grayish brown buffaloes with curved horns to pull carts and plow fields.

Birds, Bats, and Bugs

A large array of bird species are also found in the wilds of Cambodia. These include colorful parrots, peacocks, pheasants, hornbills, egrets, pelicans, and one of the fifty rarest birds in the world, the critically endangered giant ibis. This tall white bird lives in the northern wetlands of Cambodia. The giant ibis is a noisy bird that makes cranelike calls from its hook-shaped beak.

The call of the hornbill is a short bark that almost sounds like a dog.

Cambodia is also home to many different types of bats, including the fruit bat, the tomb bat, the vampire bat, the horseshoe bat, and the whisker bat. One bat called the large flying fox can be seen during the day in Phnom Penh and Siem Reap. Hundreds of these bats hang from trees, looking like strange black fruit. At sunset, they fly off in a black swarm in search of flowers and fruits to eat.

At least forty different kinds of bats live in Cambodia.

Hundreds of different types of insects live in Cambodia. Some of these insects find themselves on dinner plates in Cambodian homes. People shake trees that have ant nests to collect weaver ants. As the ants rain from the nest, a person catches them in a basket connected to a pole. The ants are cooked in a hot frying pan. Once cooked, they are crunchy with a sour taste.

Crickets are attracted to blue light. Sometimes Cambodians use blue lights to collect several gallons of crickets at night. The crickets are fried and sold in markets. They are eaten as a snack food or with rice at mealtime.

Another bug favorite is the giant spider. These large black spiders are fried and then eaten as snacks.

Thousands of Irrawaddy dolphins once thrived in the Mekong River. Today, fewer than one hundred still live in the river.

Water Animals

A well-known Cambodian expression is, "Where there is water, there is fish." Since Cambodia has a lot of water, it has a lot of fish. Mackerel, sardines, tuna, snapper, flat fish, giant Mekong River catfish, and grouper are just a few of the fish that live in the nation's waters.

Many mammals also make their home in the waters of Cambodia. These include the common dolphin, the bottle-nosed dolphin, the finless porpoise, and the dugong. The Irrawaddy dolphin is an endangered species. This dolphin can live in both freshwater and salt water. It travels in small groups and is very sociable and unafraid of humans. Its body is gray and sleek, and it looks like it has a permanent smile on its face. The Irrawaddy dolphin faces many dangers. Some fishermen on the Mekong River use explosives to kill fish, and the dolphins sometimes get caught in the blasts. Other dolphins have been killed by the sharp propellers of speedboats.

Cambodia's Poisonous Snakes

Several poisonous snake species live in Cambodia's lowlands. Though these snakes are rare, they can be deadly.

The king cobra is the world's longest poisonous snake at 18 feet (5.5 m). When frightened or excited, it rears up and expands the hood around its head. The bite of a king cobra is so deadly that it can kill an elephant.

The banded krait's entire body is covered with black and yellow stripes. This snake, which grows to 6 feet (2 m) long, mainly comes out at night. It feeds on lizards and other snakes. Since its fangs are not very long, it injects its venom by chewing on its victim.

The Russell's viper is one of the world's deadliest snakes. Its venom attacks the circulatory system and destroys muscle tissue, causing a very painful death.

The green hanuman snake is small but deadly. The snake is hard to spot because it sometimes wedges itself between stones.

Another rare creature in Cambodia is the giant royal turtle. It's called royal because the royal family ate its chicken-sized eggs as a delicacy. The turtle was once thought to be extinct. But scientists rediscovered the giant royal turtle in 2001. This turtle had not been seen alive in Cambodia since the late nineteenth century.

Trees and Plants

The plants of Cambodia vary depending on the location. The central lowlands are covered with reeds and lotus flowers.

The Strangler Fig

Unlike most trees, strangler fig trees don't grow from the ground. Instead, they sprout high on other trees' branches. The roots of the strangler fig grow down to the ground where there is water. After many years, the roots begin to grow around the host tree's trunk. Eventually, these roots strangle the host tree, and only the strangler fig is left alive. The fruits on the strangler fig tree feed monkeys and birds.

Rice, which is grown in flooded fields, and grass also grow in the lowlands. Coconut, mango, cashew nut, and orange trees flourish there as well. The "sensitive plant" also grows in the lowlands. This small bush has fernlike leaves that fold up when they are brushed.

Tall bamboo stalks, vines, and sugar palms cover Cambodia's eastern highlands. Rattan—which has a long, slender, tough stem that is used to make wicker furniture— also grows there. Giant hardwood trees such as teak and mahogany soar to the sky, reaching heights of more than 100 feet (30 m).

Pine trees blanket the upper slopes of the Cardamom and Elephant mountains. Further down the mountains, the pine forest is replaced by tropical rain forest. Finally, at the shore is a mass of twisting mangrove trees.

Tall, thin bamboo stalks are common in the forests of eastern Cambodia.

Glory and Bloodshed

CAMBODIA HAS A RICH BUT PAINFUL HISTORY. IT IS THE story of ancient glories, frequent invasions, and one of the bloodiest regimes the modern world has known. It is a story that starts some nine thousand years ago.

The oldest site in Cambodia is Laang Spean cave, which is in the northwest. Humans occupied it at various times beginning in 7000 B.C.

By about 2000 B.C., Cambodians had domesticated animals and started growing rice. By 600 B.C., they were making iron tools. Influences from India began to seep into Cambodian society by about 100 B.C.

Early Kingdoms

The Kingdom of Funan was established in Cambodia by A.D. 300. Its people were known as the Khmers. The Khmers were heavily influenced by India. As in India, Hinduism was their main religion and Sanskrit was their language.

In the sixth century, the kingdom of Funan was replaced by a new kingdom called Zhen-la. The Khmer

Opposite: **The temple of Pre Rup**

Sanskrit writing on an ancient tower in Angkor

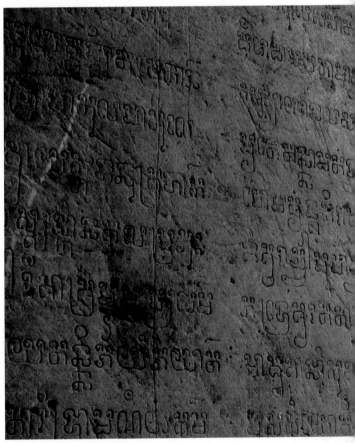

language first appeared during the Zhen-la kingdom. The religion of Buddhism was also introduced during this kingdom. It was practiced at the same time as Hinduism. At this time, Cambodia may have contained several smaller kingdoms, which battled constantly.

Angkor Kingdom

In 802, Jayavarman II came to power. He climbed to the top of a mountain called Phnom Kulen, north of modern day Siem Reap, and pronounced that he was a *devaraja*, a god-king. He demanded that the Khmer people worship him as a god. For the next 250 years, Cambodian kings claimed to be gods.

Jayavarman II wanted to make the mountain of Phnom Kulen sacred. He ordered that the river running through it be diverted. Artists carved the Hindu god Vishnu on the stony riverbed. This carving can still be seen today.

An image of King Suryavarman II is carved in a wall at Angkor Wat.

In time, the new kingdom came to be called Kambuja. This name eventually became Cambodia. Jayavarman II made Cambodia's capital Angkor and started the tradition of building temple mountains. These huge stone mountains were designed to represent Mount Meru, the place where Hindu gods lived. Walls circle the stone temples, with a moat around the outside. According to Hindu mythology, the walls around the towers symbolized the earth, and the water in the moat stood for the great ocean that surrounded Mount Meru.

Cambodia's greatest temple was built during the reign of King Suryavarman II, which started in 1112. Suryavarman built a huge temple dedicated to the Hindu god Vishnu. This temple is known as Angkor Wat—*Angkor* meaning "city" and *Wat* meaning "temple." Angkor Wat looks like a gigantic three-tiered pyramid. In the center are towers shaped like beehives that soar 181 feet (55 m) into the sky. On the outer walls are almost 2,000 elaborate carvings of *aspara* dancers, or heavenly dancing girls. The inner walls are covered with scenes from King Suryavarman II's life.

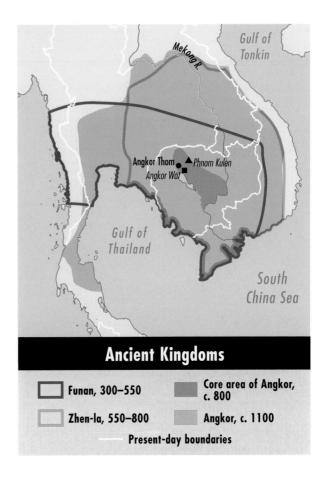

Ancient Kingdoms

Funan, 300–550

Zhen-la, 550–800

Core area of Angkor, c. 800

Angkor, c. 1100

Present-day boundaries

In 1177, rebels from the Cham region sacked the temple, and a Cham prince was put on the throne. But soon, King Jayavarman VII drove the Chams out. He then built a beautiful city called Angkor Thom. Two of the city's gates were crowned with four large stone faces. At the center of Angkor Thom was a huge temple called the Bayon. This temple has about fifty towers, many with four giant carved faces on the top. On the lower walls are carvings of everyday life. These carvings show everything from battle scenes to pig roasts to villagers picking lice from each other's hair.

The Temples of Angkor

From the ninth to the thirteenth centuries, Khmer kings usually began their reign by building a new temple. As a result, more than one hundred temples were built. The temples were the spiritual and cultural heart of Cambodia. At first, the temples were influenced by India's art and religion. The older temples have stone images of Hindu gods (above). Later, when Buddhism became more popular, carvings of Buddha were made. Today, the temple ruins of the Angkor kingdom cover about 75 square miles (200 sq km).

Siam and Vietnam Invade

After King Jayavarman VII died in about 1219, the Khmer Empire went into decline. In 1431, Siam, the country now known as Thailand, captured the capital of Angkor Thom. The Khmer then moved their capital to Phnom Penh. For the next four centuries, Cambodia was frequently invaded by both the Siamese and the Vietnamese.

By the 1800s, the Vietnamese ruled the central part of the country. They forced the Cambodians to accept Vietnamese traditions. Cambodians found this oppressive, and uprisings flared up in 1840 and 1841. After two years of battles, Cambodian, Siamese, and Vietnamese leaders agreed that the country would be under equal rule of both Siam and Vietnam. Both countries saw the need for Cambodia to have a king, so a new monarch, Ang Duong, was placed on the throne.

Ang Duong was crowned Cambodia's king in 1848. During his rule, Cambodia experienced a decade of peace and some independence. Even so, King Ang Duong feared that the monarchy would not continue in Cambodia. He asked the Siamese king to allow his son, Prince Norodom, to be given

Phnom Penh in 1867

Revealing Angkor

After the Khmer left Angkor, the temples fell into ruin. Jungle plants and huge banyan trees covered them. It would be hundreds of years before the glories of Angkor became known in the western world.

In 1860, Henri Mouhot (right), a French naturalist, visited the ancient ruins. When Mouhot asked the locals who built the enormous ruins, the reply was, "Who else but giants, or the king of angels?"

Mouhot's writings about the ruins became famous. Though other Europeans had come to Angkor before him, Mouhot's powerful writing and evocative drawings of the ruins captured the imagination of his fellow Europeans.

the title of *Obbareach*, which meant that he was the recognized heir to the throne. This would ensure that when Ang Duong died, his son would succeed him on the throne.

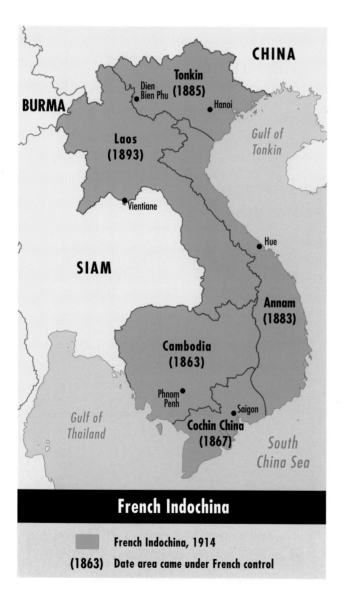

CHINA

Tonkin (1885)

Dien Bien Phu

Hanoi

BURMA

Gulf of Tonkin

Laos (1893)

Vientiane

Hue

SIAM

Annam (1883)

Cambodia (1863)

Phnom Penh

Saigon

Gulf of Thailand

Cochin China (1867)

South China Sea

French Indochina

French Indochina, 1914

(1863)   Date area came under French control

French Rule

King Ang Duong was concerned that the Vietnamese and Siamese would tear Cambodia apart. So in 1855, he sent a letter to the French asking for their protection. The Protectorate Treaty with France wasn't signed until 1863. By this time, Ang Duong's son Norodom was on the throne.

The Protectorate Treaty gave France the power to control Cambodia's relations with other countries. In return, France pledged to honor the Cambodian king, to protect Cambodia from foreign attack, and to help maintain order within the country. In 1887, the French forced King Norodom to accept complete French control of Cambodia, which became part of French Indochina. During their rule, the French did little to educate the Cambodians. Instead, they built roads and encouraged the growth of export products such as rubber, corn, and rice.

The Independence Monument

Built in 1958, the Independence Monument in Phnom Penh commemorates the end of French rule in Cambodia. It also serves as a memorial to the Cambodians who laid down their lives fighting for freedom. The monument's design is Angkorian. It has five levels decorated with a hundred snakeheads.

Many years later, in 1941, the French government chose eighteen-year-old Norodom Sihanouk to reign as king. They thought his youth would make him easy to manipulate. But within eleven years, the feisty young ruler wrote several letters to the president of France, demanding Cambodia's independence. By 1953, he got his way. Cambodia regained its independence from the French.

Two years later, Sihanouk made another brave move. He gave up the throne and formed a political party. Elections were held, and Sihanouk's party won every seat in the National Assembly. Sihanouk was elected prime minister.

Recent Kings of Cambodia

1848–1859	King Ang Duong
1859–1904	King Norodom
1904–1927	King Sisowath
1927–1941	King Sisowath Monivong
1941–1955	King Norodom Sihanouk (first time)
1955–1960	King Norodom Suramarit
1993–2004	King Norodom Sihanouk (second time)
2004–	King Norodam Sihamoni

Troubled Years

Sihanouk remained a popular leader through the 1960s. But by the late 1960s, his popularity was dwindling. At the time, the United States was fighting the communist government in North Vietnam over control of South Vietnam. Sihanouk aligned himself with the North Vietnamese and allowed them to set up bases in Cambodia. Sihanouk also cut ties with the United States.

Cambodia was also troubled at home. Sihanouk had set up a highly praised education program, but jobs were scarce. In addition, prices for Cambodia's main exports, rice and rubber, were dropping. Discontent rumbled throughout the country. In 1970, one of Sihanouk's formerly loyal supporters, General Lon Nol, overthrew Sihanouk.

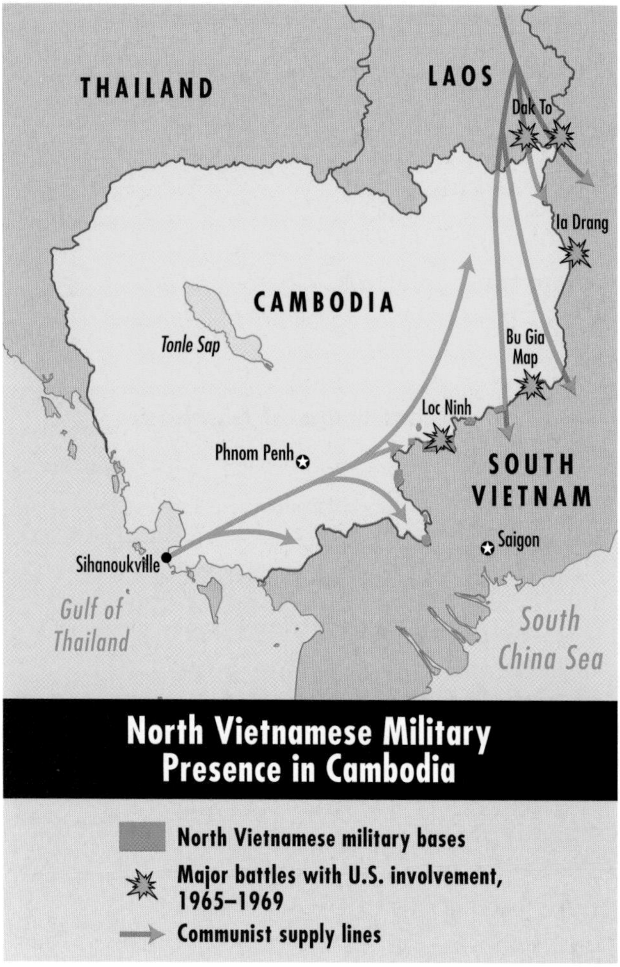

Lon Nol immediately went to work establishing ties with the United States. He gave the United States permission to bomb the North Vietnamese bases in Cambodia. The bombing campaign destroyed the bases. It also killed about half a million Cambodians. Many Cambodians were filled with rage at the United States and at Lon Nol. They began supporting an unofficial army called the Khmer Rouge, which was led by a communist named Pol Pot.

By 1975, Pol Pot's forces had overthrown Lon Nol's government. Pol Pot's new government was called Democratic Kampuchea. His plan was to turn Cambodia into a rice-growing machine. The entire country was turned into government-owned collective farms.

North Vietnamese Military Presence in Cambodia

- North Vietnamese military bases
- Major battles with U.S. involvement, 1965–1969
- Communist supply lines

Map labels: THAILAND, LAOS, Dak To, Ia Drang, CAMBODIA, Tonle Sap, Bu Gia Map, Loc Ninh, Phnom Penh, SOUTH VIETNAM, Saigon, Sihanoukville, Gulf of Thailand, South China Sea

The Great Heroic King Sihanouk

Norodom Sihanouk was born on October 31, 1922, in Phnom Penh. In 1941, when he was eighteen years old, the French appointed him king. In 1952, he started a "royal crusade for independence" by writing letters to the French government to withdraw their forces from Cambodia. He demanded complete independence, and by 1953, France announced its withdrawal. King Sihanouk became known as the Father of Cambodian Independence.

By 1955, Sihanouk started a new political party called the People's Socialist Community. Elections were held in September 1955, and Sihanouk became prime minister. In that position, he tried to improve education and health care.

After being overthrown by General Lon Nol in 1970, Sihanouk fled to China. From China, he supported the efforts of a communist group in Cambodia called the Khmer Rouge. When the Khmer Rouge took control of Cambodia, King Sihanouk returned, but he was immediately placed under house arrest in Phnom Penh.

The Vietnamese defeated the Khmer Rouge in 1979, and King Sihanouk returned to China. He lived there until 1990. In 1991, he successfully negotiated a peace agreement with all warring parties in Cambodia. He

was able to return to his beloved country. In 1993, he once again was named king.

Sihanouk decided to abdicate, or give up, his right to the throne in 2004 because of his poor health. Today, he is called the Great Heroic King Sihanouk.

The first act of the Khmer Rouge after they gained power was to evacuate large cities. The two million people living in Phnom Penh were forced to abandon their homes and live in the countryside. After the evacuation, Phnom Penh was like a ghost town.

Nearly all Cambodians were forced to work as slave labor in rice fields. The punishment for disobeying a Khmer Rouge soldier was often death. The Khmer Rouge abolished money and education. Anyone with an education was in danger of being killed. The Khmer Rouge killed engineers, doctors, factory workers, Buddhist monks, artists, and students. Because they saw city people as enemies, they also sometimes killed people who wore glasses or who had smooth skin on their hands. These were signs that they were not loyal farmers.

It is estimated that the Khmer Rouge killed one million to two million Cambodians between 1975 and 1979. More than

The Tuol Sleng Genocide Museum

Tuol Sleng was originally a high school. In 1975, the Khmer Rouge turned it into an interrogation and execution center. The Khmer Rouge put up iron sheets covered with electrified barbed wire around the complex. This was to prevent any of the prisoners from escaping. The classrooms were divided into cells sized 2.5 feet by 6.5 feet (0.8 m by 2 m). Prisoners were shackled with chains to the wall or floor.

People from many nations were held at Tuol Sleng, including Americans, Canadians, and Britons. But the majority of prisoners were Cambodian. The prisoners came from a variety of backgrounds. They included teachers, ministers, diplomats, and engineers. Many of the guards were young children from ages ten to fifteen. Their training by the Khmer Rouge turned these normal children into exceptionally cruel and heartless guards.

It is estimated that more than thirteen thousand prisoners were killed at Tuol Sleng. Today, the building is maintained as a museum to remind people of the cruelties that took place under the Khmer Rouge.

Many thousands of people were killed and buried in mass graves during the reign of the Khmer Rouge.

thirteen thousand people were killed at an interrogation camp called Tuol Sleng. They were buried near a farm outside Phnom Penh. These grounds became known as the Killing Fields. Such mass graves have been found around the country.

Children raised in Cambodia during the Khmer Rouge years were taught to hate family. They learned that the ruling party would take care of them. Religion was abolished. Buddhist temples were turned into warehouses or stables. All Islamic mosques and Catholic churches were destroyed.

Vietnam invaded Cambodia in December 1978. On January 7, 1979, Phnom Penh was captured, and the Khmer Rouge leaders fled. The Vietnamese set up a new government called the People's Republic of Kampuchea. Under Vietnamese rule, religion was allowed to return.

Clearing the Land Mines of Cambodia

Many millions of land mines were planted in Cambodia during its thirty years of civil war. It is estimated that 10 million are still in the ground, ready to go off. Though a mine is a weapon of war, it cannot tell the difference between soldier, child, woman, or animal. Anyone who steps on a land mine may have their leg blown off or even be killed.

Charitable organizations in Cambodia have begun the huge task of removing the land mines. This is very slow, dangerous work. People searching for mines begin their day using metal detectors. Each time they find metal, they have to determine if it is a mine. If it is, the mine is marked. They continue all day, marking mines in a straight path. Then, before they leave in the evening, the marked mines are blown up.

With the collapse of the Khmer Rouge regime, refugees poured into Thailand, where they lived in makeshift camps. Many fled Southeast Asia, moving to countries such as the United States, Canada, Australia, France, and Spain.

Though the Vietnamese were now in control of the country, the Khmer Rouge still did not surrender. They set up bases in northwestern Cambodia. Their last final strongholds were the central Cardamom Mountains and the Dangrek Mountains. People avoided these areas through the 1990s because the Khmer Rouge sometimes kidnapped or killed intruders. They had also planted millions of land mines in the ground. These mines blow up when someone steps on them.

In 1989, the Vietnamese withdrew their troops from Cambodia. In 1991, four warring factions, or groups, in Cambodia signed a peace plan. A cease-fire was declared, and all Cambodian refugees in Thailand were told to return to Cambodia. The first elections in twenty years were held in May 1993. The Khmer Rouge leaders finally surrendered in 1998, and peace was restored.

No one in Cambodia would ever forget the crimes of the Khmer Rouge. But many leaders of the Khmer Rouge continued living freely in the country. The public began demanding that the Khmer Rouge leaders be put on trial for the millions of people they killed. The government has begun planning for trials, but so far, none has taken place. And as the years go by, the elderly Khmer Rouge leaders are dying. Pol Pot himself died without ever having been brought to justice.

Ta Mok, a leader of the Khmer Rouge, was captured in 1998. In 2005, he still had not been tried for his crimes of thirty years earlier.

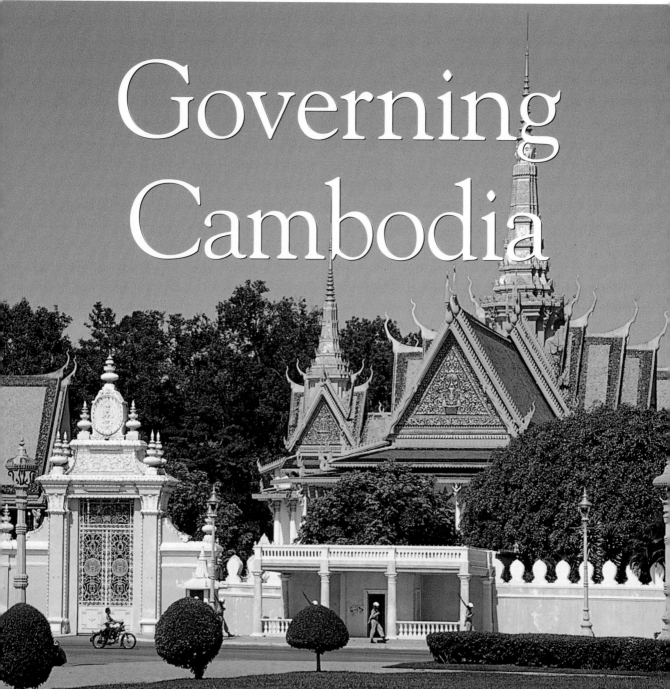

Governing Cambodia

C AMBODIA'S OFFICIAL NAME IS THE KINGDOM OF
Cambodia. It is a constitutional monarchy. This means that
the nation has a king, but that he must follow the laws and
principles of the constitution of Cambodia.

Cambodia's constitution was approved in 1993. It defines
the role and powers of the king of Cambodia. It also outlines
the government structure and the rights and duties of
Cambodian citizens, such as voting rights, ownership rights,
and equal rights for men and women.

Opposite: **The Royal Palace in Phnom Penh**

Cambodia's National Flag

The Cambodian flag has a picture of Angkor Wat in its center. The temple has been on the flag since the 1800s. The color and style of the flag, however, has varied depending on which political party was in power.

The Khmer Rouge ruled Cambodia from 1975 to 1979. During this time, the flag had a red background with three yellow towers. The flag of the People's Republic of Kampuchea, from 1979 to 1989, had a red background with five yellow towers. The flag of the noncommunist forces had a blue and red background with white towers. This flag was reinstated in 1993.

The three colors of the Cambodian flag represent different parts of the government. The blue bands signify the royalty of Cambodia. The red band and the red outline of Angkor Wat stand for the nation. The white of the temple symbolizes Buddhism, the religion of Cambodia. These three colors also represent the motto of the Khmer monarchy, "King, Nation, and Religion."

Crowning a King

The coronation of a Cambodian king can take place over several days, months, or even years. Certain sacred objects are used during the ceremony. They are called royal regalia.

The Great Crown of Victory is a multitiered cone made of gold and jewels. Its pointed top is supposed to represent the sacred Mount Meru. The Great White Umbrella of State is made of nine tiered white silk umbrellas sewed together with gold thread. The Sacred Sword and the Victory Spear are rumored to have existed before the Angkor kingdom. But scientists think it is more likely that they were made in the sixteenth century. The Sacred Sword is made of gold and silver. The Victory Spear is cast in iron. The Slippers are flat shoes made of gold. They are very heavy.

These are just a few of the items used when Cambodia crowns a king. In October 2004, Cambodia crowned a new king, Norodom Sihamoni.

The King and His Powers

Only certain people can become king of Cambodia. To become king, a person must be a member of the royal family and be descended from the bloodline of King Ang Duong, King Norodom, or King Sisowath. He must also be at least thirty years old. When the king dies or becomes unable to perform his duties, a new king is appointed.

The king does not have the right to choose who succeeds him. Instead, the Royal Council of the Throne chooses the new king. This council consists of the president of the Senate, the president of the National Assembly, the prime minister, the first and second vice presidents of the assembly, the first and second vice presidents of the Senate, and leaders of the country's two large Buddhist groups.

The king of Cambodia is appointed head of state for life, and his position is considered sacred. He does not have the power to rule or govern his people. But he is a strong symbol of the unity among the Cambodian people and the longevity of the Kingdom of Cambodia.

The king alone is given the responsibility to ensure Cambodia remains an independent country and free from foreign rule. The king also oversees and protects the rights and freedoms for all Cambodian citizens.

Cambodia's Newest King

King Norodom Sihamoni was born on May 14, 1953, in Phnom Penh. His parents were King Norodom Sihanouk and Queen Norodom Monineath Sihanouk. He attended school for a few years in Phnom Penh, but most of his schooling was in Prague, in what is now the Czech Republic. Sihamoni studied dance, music, and theater at the Academy of Musical Art of Prague.

For nineteen years, he served as a professor of classical dance and artistic teaching in Paris, France. Also during this time, he was the president of the Khmer Dance Association in France and a permanent representative of Cambodia to the United Nations. Sihamoni is fluent in many languages, including Khmer, French, English, and Czech.

Sihamoni was given the title of Great Prince on February 1, 1994. Ten years later, his father, King Sihanouk, began suffering poor health and announced that he would like to retire. On October 14, 2004, Norodom Sihamoni was elected unanimously by the members of the Royal Council of the Throne as the new king of Cambodia.

A meeting of the Cambodian National Assembly

The Cambodian Government

The executive branch in the Cambodian government is made up of the king, who is the head of state, and the prime minister, who is the head of government. The cabinet, which is called the Council of Ministers, is part of the executive branch.

Cambodia also has two lawmaking bodies, the National Assembly and the Senate. The National Assembly consists of 123 members who are elected by popular vote for a five-year term. The members of the National Assembly choose the prime minister. The Senate has sixty-one members. Two of its members are appointed by the king, two are elected by the National Assembly, and fifty-seven are elected by special election groups called functional constituencies. Each senator serves a five-year term.

In Cambodia, most of the power lies within the executive branch. The National Assembly passes the laws but does not have enough power to stop the actions of the executive branch.

The Judicial System

Several different courts make up Cambodia's judicial system. The Courts of First Instance are the courts in every province and city around the country. Appeals courts are above the Courts of First Instance. The highest court in the land is the Supreme Court. The Supreme Council of the Magistracy is responsible for appointing, overseeing, and disciplining judges throughout Cambodia.

Trials in Cambodia are public. According to the constitution, a person accused of a crime has the right to be present at the trial and to consult with an attorney. Defendants can also confront and question witnesses against

Cambodia's National Anthem

"Nokoreach" ("Royal Kingdom") was adopted as Cambodia's national anthem in 1941. It was not used during much of the country's long civil war, but it was restored as the national anthem in 1993.

Heaven protects our King
And gives him happiness and glory
To reign over our souls and our destinies,
The one being, heir of the Sovereign builders,
Guiding the proud old Kingdom.

Temples are asleep in the forest,
Remembering the splendour of Moha Nokor.
Like a rock the Khmer race is eternal.
Let us trust in the fate of Kampuchea,
The empire which challenges the ages.

Songs rise up from the pagodas
To the glory of the holy Buddhistic faith.
Let us be faithful to our ancestors' beliefs.
Thus heaven will lavish its bounty
Towards the ancient Khmer country, the Moha Nokor.

A group of men stand as they go on trial for their actions during a violent political demonstration.

NATIONAL GOVERNMENT OF CAMBODIA

Executive Branch

The King

Prime Minister

Senate (61 members)

Legislative Branch

National Assembly (123 members)

Senate (61 members)

Judicial Branch

Supreme Court

Courts of Appeal

Courts of First Instance

them and present witnesses and evidence on their behalf. Despite these rights, most defendants in Cambodia do not have lawyers. Partly this is because the country has very few lawyers. It is also because most people in Cambodia are too poor to afford a lawyer's services.

Recent Politics

Many different political parties vie for power in Cambodia. Three parties currently dominate. One is the Cambodian People's Party, or CPP, led by Prime Minister Hun Sen. The second is the National United Front for an Independent, Neutral, Peaceful, and Cooperative Cambodia, which is known as FUNCINPEC, after the first letters in its name in French. FUNCINPEC is led by Prince Norodom Ranariddh, the son of the king. The last main party is the Sam Rainsy Party, or SRP, led by Sam Rainsy. Many smaller parties also participate in elections. In 2003, twenty-three parties were on the ballot.

Though Cambodia now has a constitution, it still faces frequent political upheaval. In 1997, Hun Sen and Norodom Ranariddh were co-prime ministers. Then Hun Sen decided to take control of the government and throw Norodom Ranariddh out. As a result, hundreds of people were killed. Despite this violence, elections were held on schedule in 1998. After Hun Sen's CPP won the elections, violent protests again erupted. In the end, the CPP and FUNCINPEC formed a coalition, or combined, government.

Because of this violent history, several international groups kept a close eye on Cambodia's 2003 elections. These organizations wanted to ensure that the elections were fair and democratic.

Norodom Ranariddh leads FUNCINPEC, one of Cambodia's leading political parties.

Leading up to the elections, signs were nailed to trees and boards. Party supporters were given T-shirts and hats. Supporters were then loaded into open-bed trucks or boats with megaphones. Starting at 6 A.M., they sang songs, chanted, and yelled to promote their party while driving down the street or floating along the Tonle Sap.

The 2003 elections went much more smoothly than the 1998 elections, but abuses still occurred. Some village chiefs told the residents that if they didn't vote for the Cambodian People's Party, they might lose their land or be kicked out of the village. Some people were also threatened when they attempted to put up signs for their party.

Cambodia's Prime Minister

Hun Sen is prime minister of Cambodia. He was a member of the Khmer Rouge in the 1970s. But after seeing the atrocities committed by the Khmer Rouge, he fled to Vietnam in 1977. After the Vietnamese invaded Cambodia in 1979, Hun Sen became the foreign minister in the new government.

By 1985, Hun Sen was the most powerful figure in the Cambodian government. After national elections in 1993, Hun Sen and Prince Norodom Ranariddh became co-prime ministers and formed a coalition government. Hun Sen was elected sole prime minister in the 1998 elections and again in the 2003 elections. After each election, Hun Sen, leader of the CPP, formed a coalition government with Prince Norodom Ranariddh, leader of FUNCINPEC.

A man casts his vote during the 2003 election.

On July 27, 2003, more than 6.3 million voters showed up to cast their ballots. When the ballots were finally counted, the CPP was announced as the winner. While the CPP won a majority of the vote, they did not have the two-thirds majority required by the constitution to form a government. For almost a year, no new government was formed. Finally, in July 2004, FUNCINPEC agreed to form a new coalition government with the CPP. This shut out the Sam Rainsy Party that had come in second in the popular vote.

Phnom Penh: Did You Know This?

The capital city of Cambodia is Phnom Penh, which is located where the Mekong, Tonle Sap, and Bassac Rivers branch. The bustling capital is the center of culture, economy, society, and politics in Cambodia. In 1998, it had a population of 999,804.

Phnom Penh means the "hill of Penh." Cambodians have a legend about how Phnom Penh began. They say that a lady named Penh lived on a hill in the small village. One day, she found a huge tree floating in the river. Inside the tree trunk, she found statues of Buddha, the founder of Buddhism. Lady Penh soon became busy building a temple on her hill to house the statues.

During the time of the Angkor kingdom, Phnom Penh was just a small village. After Angkor was invaded, the Cambodian capital moved to Longuck and then Oudong, before settling at Phnom Penh.

Today, Phnom Penh is the site of the Royal Palace (above), the residence of the king. The roof of the palace is covered with golden yellow tiles that glimmer in the afternoon sun. The main living quarters are never open to visitors, but the throne room and other buildings can be visited.

The Silver Pagoda sits on the grounds of the Royal Palace. Its floor is covered with 5,000 silver tiles. The pagoda is famed for its life-size solid gold Buddha covered with diamonds and for a green crystal Buddha.

Phnom Penh is warm year-round. Its average daily temperature in January is 78.9°F (26.1°C). In July, it is 80.6°F (27.0°C). The rainy season runs from May to November. October is the wettest month.

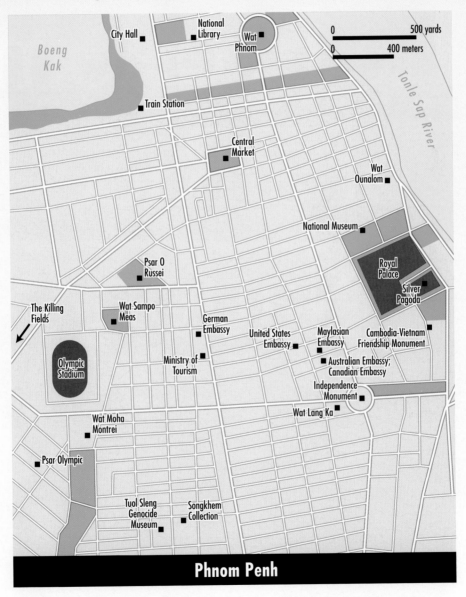

Phnom Penh

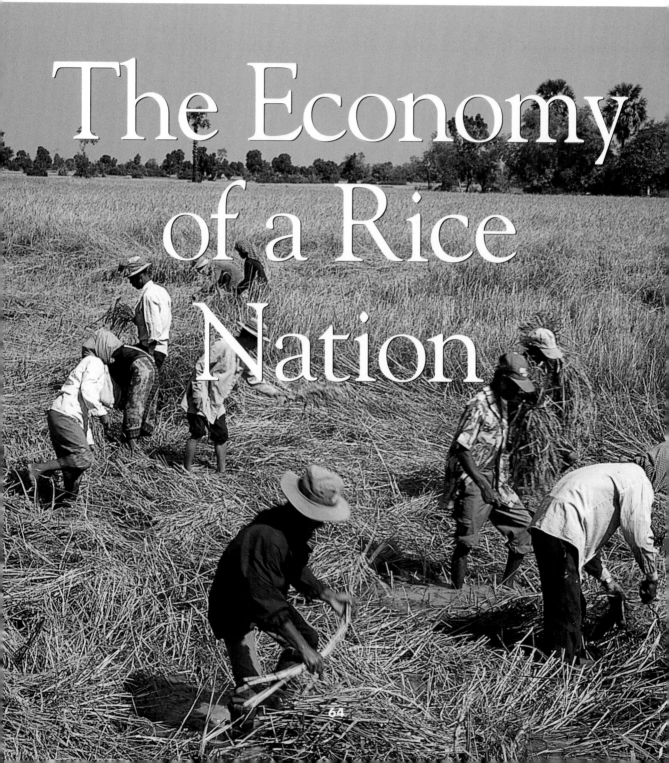

The Economy of a Rice Nation

CAMBODIA IS ONE OF THE POOREST COUNTRIES IN THE world. Years of civil war and strife left many people in the country impoverished. Today, the Cambodian economy is slowly reviving.

Agriculture

Agriculture is the largest part of Cambodia's economy. It makes up 36.6 percent of the gross domestic product, or all the goods and services produced by the country. More than 75 percent of Cambodia's labor force work in agriculture. Most are rice farmers.

Most Cambodians are farmers.

Weights and Measures

Cambodia's system of weights and measurements is the metric system. In this system, 1 meter is equal to 39.37 inches, and 1 kilogram is equal to 2.2 pounds.

Rice has been the most important crop in Cambodia for hundreds of years. Carvings on ancient temple walls show Khmers growing and harvesting rice, and it remains an important staple in the Cambodian diet today. It is eaten at least twice a day. Rice crops are grown twice a year in Cambodia, during the dry season and the rainy season.

More than half the farmland in Cambodia is planted with rice. Many different varieties of rice seeds are now planted. During the reign of the Khmer Rouge, however, the government controlled rice production, and they used only a few rice varieties. Other rice varieties were lost. After the Khmer Rouge fell from power, the International Rice Research Institute (IRRI) reintroduced 766 varieties of rice into Cambodia. The IRRI is an agricultural research and training center that helps rice farmers, especially those with low incomes.

Rice production has varied over the years. After civil war broke out in Cambodia in 1970, the country's annual rice production dropped dramatically, from 4 million tons to as low as 50,000 tons. Since peace was restored, rice production has climbed to even higher than it was. Cambodia now produces more than 4 million tons of rice each year, enough to export some of it.

The Fishing Industry

Another main food item in Cambodia is fish. Fisher families live along the Mekong River and the Tonle Sap. They use nets, cages, baskets, and homemade traps to catch the abundant fish in the waters. Some Cambodians also fish in the ocean.

Just as rice was important to ancient Khmers, so were fish. Carvings on temple walls depict fishing scenes on the Tonle Sap. Today, most of Cambodia's freshwater fish come from the Tonle Sap. It is one of the largest fisheries in the world.

A man uses a basket to fish in the Tonle Sap.

What Cambodia Grows and Makes

Agriculture (2001)

Rice	4,099,016 metric tons
Fish	444,500 metric tons
Corn	343,241 metric tons

Manufacturing (value added in U.S. dollars)

Wood Products	$9,858,000 (2002)
Food Products	$2,758,567 (1997)
Garment Industry Products	$1,147,000 (2001)

Other Natural Resources

Cambodia's forests are an important natural resource, but in recent years they have been shrinking. In 1969, 75 percent of Cambodia was covered with forests. By 1993, that number had dropped to 49 percent.

There are many reasons for this. Many rural Cambodians use timber as fuel. Also, during the time of the Khmer Rouge, the entire population of Cambodia was moved to rural areas. To make room for all these people, forests were cleared and houses built. Illegal logging is probably the biggest reason for the forest's decline. Most of the timber that is cut illegally is sold to Hong Kong, China, Taiwan, and Japan.

Clearing Cambodia's forestland has affected the Mekong River. Flooding is more common during the wet season, and less water flows in the dry season.

Gemstones are another of Cambodia's natural treasures. Red rubies and dark blue sapphires have been mined there. Chinese and French scientists have stated that Cambodia has vast amounts of gemstones. But

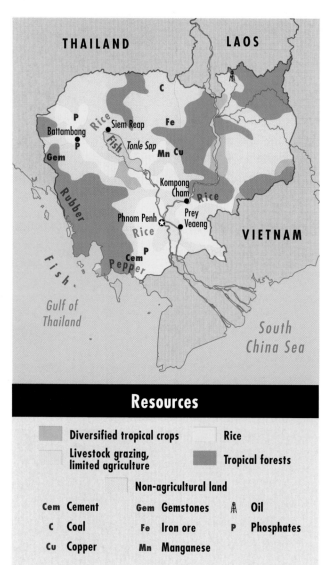

Resources

- Diversified tropical crops
- Rice
- Livestock grazing, limited agriculture
- Tropical forests
- Non-agricultural land

Cem	Cement	Gem	Gemstones	Oil
C	Coal	Fe	Iron ore	P Phosphates
Cu	Copper	Mn	Manganese	

Two percent of Cambodia's forests are being cut down every year. Most of this logging is illegal.

Workers dig rubies and sapphires from a mine in Cambodia.

because of the nation's many years of war and internal struggle, gemstones have not been as extensively mined there as in other countries.

Historically, rubber was an important export product in Cambodia. The onset of the civil war in 1970 put most rubber farms out of business, however. In recent years, the industry has been slowly recovering, and Cambodia is once again exporting rubber. Today, Cambodia produces about 40,000 tons of rubber per year.

Cambodia also produces small amounts of cement, coal, copper, oil, iron, manganese, and phosphates.

Money Facts

The Cambodian unit of currency is the riel. It comes in notes from 50 riel to 50,000. There is also a 100,000-riel note, but it is rare. Many stores now refuse to take 50-riel notes because they are worth so little. In February 2005, 4,002 Cambodian riel was equal to 1 U.S. dollar.

Tourism

Services, which include tourism, make up 36.4 percent of the gross domestic product. Tourism is Cambodia's fastest-growing industry. Tourists shied away from Cambodia for many years because of its political instability. Since peace has been restored, the number of tourists has been increasing by about 30 percent a year.

A growing number of tourists are traveling to Cambodia to marvel at its ancient temples.

Pictures on the Riel

Riel notes are quite colorful, with pictures on both sides. Most of the pictures relate to Cambodian history and everyday life. The 100-riel note, for instance, has a picture of the Independence Monument on one side and a school on the other. Other notes have pictures of Angkor Wat, King Sihanouk, dragon boat races, bridges, construction workers, and rice fields.

Imports and Exports

Cambodia imports more products than it exports, meaning Cambodia buys more goods from other countries than it sells to other countries.

Among the products Cambodia exports are timber, clothing, rubber, rice, and fish. Its biggest export partner is the United States. Many basic items, such as construction materials, machinery, and cars, are not produced in Cambodia. The country imports the most goods from Singapore and Thailand.

Construction workers build a school outside Phnom Penh.

Common Items in a Store in Cambodia

A loaf of bread	500 riel (US$0.14)
1 kg (2.2 lb.) of rice	700 riel (US$0.19)
1 kg (2.2 lb.) of pig's feet	9,000 riel (US$2.43)
1 kg (2.2 lb.) of beef	9,000 riel (US$2.43)
A dozen chicken eggs	3,000 riel (US$0.81)
1 soda pop	3,000 riel (US$0.81)

Making a Living

Making a living in Cambodia is difficult. Workers get paid very little. A recent survey found that waiters and waitresses make just 2,473 riel per day (about 50 cents) and rice field workers make 4,400 riel per day (a little more than $1). Construction is one of the higher-paying jobs, with workers making 14,891 riel per day (almost $4).

Cambodia has six main television stations and twenty-five cable television stations. The six main stations are National Television of Kampuchea, Royal Army Television, Phnom Penh's Municipal Television, Apsara Television, Khmer Television, and Bayon Television. Cambodia also has nineteen radio stations.

Many newspapers are published in Cambodia. There are 160 newspapers written in Khmer and 36 newspapers written in foreign languages such as English and French. The major daily newspapers are *Cambodia Daily* (English and Khmer); *Raksmei Kampuchea*, which means "light of Cambodia"; *Koh Santepheap*, which means "peace island"; *Samleng Yuvachun*,

Cambodia has many news outlets. Here, reporters question Norodom Sihanouk upon his return from exile.

which means "youth voice"; and *Ma-nac Seka*, which means "conscience."

Prior to the 1970s, Cambodia was very active in the movie industry and made a number of high-quality films. These achievements were literally erased during the time of the Khmer Rouge. Since 1992, the film industry has started up again. One movie titled *Konpous Keng Kang*, or *Baby Snake*, became very popular.

Even though Cambodia is rapidly becoming a modern country, few people use the Internet. In 2002, Cambodia had about 30,000 Internet users. Computers are too expensive for most Cambodians to own. Most of the nation's Internet users are government workers, businesspeople, and students. Visitors to Cambodia can log on at Internet cafés in Phnom Penh, Battambang, Kompong Cham, Siem Reap, and Sihanoukville.

Actors playing fifteenth-century soldiers charge up a hill. Filmmaking is a growing industry in Cambodia.

Air travel is the fastest way to get in and out of Cambodia.

Transportation

There are four different ways to travel in Cambodia—by air, water, road, and rail—but some are faster than others. Cambodia has two international airports, the Pochentong International Airport in Phnom Penh and the Siem Reap International Airport. Both airports have been renovated recently and are very modern. In total, Cambodia has twenty airports scattered throughout the country, five with paved runways.

As of 2005, Cambodia had a number of domestic and regional airlines and four major airlines. The four major airines are Royal Phnom Penh Airways, President Airlines, Mekong Airlines, and Siem Reap Airlines.

Travel is slow on Cambodia's rough, unpaved roads.

The river system in Cambodia makes boat travel easy. With many established water routes to major cities, traveling by boat would seem like the perfect option. During the rainy season, ferries and ships transfer products such as timber, food, and household goods. But trips may be delayed in the dry season because of low water. Oxcarts sometimes replace boats along streams that cannot be navigated during the dry season. The main seaport in Cambodia is Sihanoukville, and the main river port is Phnom Penh.

In 1970, Cambodia had seven major roads. These roads were severely damaged during the country's years of warfare. In many cases, all that remained of the roads was deep sand, broken rock, muddy swamps, and damaged bridges. But this is changing. International funding is helping rebuild the roads. Today, the best roads in Cambodia are National Road No. 4, which runs from Phnom Penh to Sihanoukville, and National

Road No. 6, which runs from Phnom Penh to Kompang Cham. National Road No. 1, which runs from the Vietnamese border to Phnom Penh, is currently under construction.

Cambodians sometimes carry huge amounts of goods on their scooters.

Cars and scooters buzz around on the streets of major cities. Sometimes families of four or five people cram onto one scooter, clinging to each other. Some scooters pull trailers, which may have seats for passengers. Other trailers are more like truck beds and are used to haul just about anything, including wood, pigs, rice, and bamboo baskets. These are called *ra moks*.

Cambodia has just two railroad lines. The trains are extremely slow and uncomfortable and can take many hours to arrive at their destination. Many people cram into railcars. Sometimes the cars are so crowded that people sit on the roofs or hang out the windows.

Living Together

ALL CAMBODIANS HAVE LIVED THROUGH DIFFICULT times. Violence and poverty have been the rule rather than the exception. But many Cambodians are trying to put the past behind them, and the country is slowly progressing toward an era of peace and increasing prosperity.

Cambodians have proven themselves a strong and resolute people. They welcome visitors with open arms.

Opposite: **Cambodian girls**

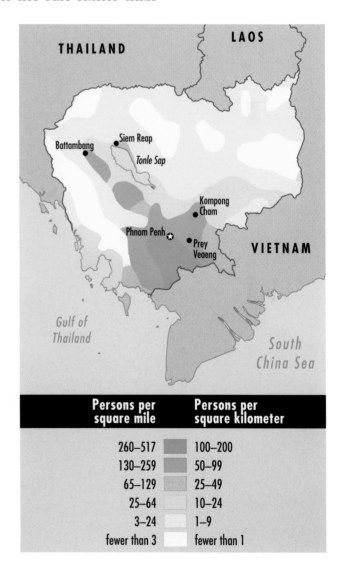

Persons per square mile	Persons per square kilometer
260–517	100–200
130–259	50–99
65–129	25–49
25–64	10–24
3–24	1–9
fewer than 3	fewer than 1

The Population

Cambodia is home to more than 13 million people. Most people in Cambodia are Khmers. The Khmers are one of the oldest ethnic groups in Southeast Asia. Khmers are slightly taller than the neighboring Thais and have round, dark brown eyes and black hair.

The Vietnamese are the second-largest ethnic group in Cambodia. It is hard to know how many Vietnamese live in Cambodia. Some have lived there for generations. Others have just

Population of Cambodia's Largest Provinces (1998)

Kompong Cham	1,608,914
Kandal	1,075,125
Prey Veaeng	946,042
Battambang	793,129
Takaev	790,168
Siem Reap	696,164

arrived. Many Vietnamese are fishermen who live in floating villages around the Tonle Sap lake. Historically, the Vietnamese and the Khmer have disliked and distrusted one another. Their relations have been colored by violence. Vietnam has invaded Cambodia several times. The Khmer Rouge killed many Vietnamese who were living in Cambodia. But every stereotype has exceptions. Some Khmers and Vietnamese are good friends.

A Vietnamese grocery store on the Tonle Sap

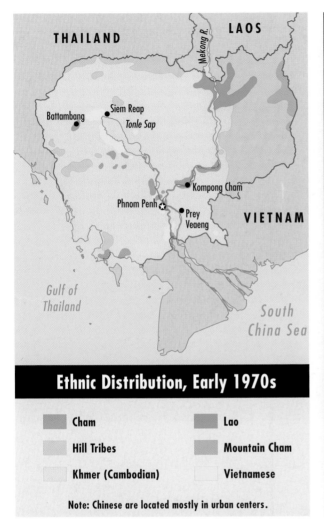

Ethnic Distribution, Early 1970s

- Cham
- Hill Tribes
- Khmer (Cambodian)
- Lao
- Mountain Cham
- Vietnamese

Note: Chinese are located mostly in urban centers.

A young Muslim woman

Many Chinese also live in Cambodia. They are often merchants and traders who contribute much to Cambodia's economy. The Chinese and Khmers mix well and often intermarry.

Another smaller ethnic group in Cambodia are the Chams. They are Muslims rather than Buddhists. The Chams live on the shores of the Mekong River. Many make a living by fishing, raising cattle, and building boats.

Most members of the hill tribes live in the mountains of northeast Cambodia.

Smaller groups known as the hill tribes live in the mountainous regions of Cambodia. Most live in the northeast near the border with Laos. Their language, customs, dress, and religious beliefs are different from the Khmer.

The People of Cambodia

Khmer	90%
Vietnamese	5%
Chinese	1%
Chams, hill tribes, Europeans, and others	4%

Education

Not everyone in Cambodia goes to school. Outside of the major cities, there is usually only one primary school for every two to three villages. Some parts of Cambodia have no schools at all. As a result, about half of all women and one-quarter of all men there cannot read or write.

In the bigger cities, some children attend preschool. But most children start attending school at age six or seven. Primary school covers grades one through six. Grades seven through nine are called lower secondary school. Once students complete lower secondary school, they must pass an exam to continue on to upper secondary school, which is grades ten through twelve.

The country has few secondary schools, so most Cambodians attend only primary school. Some of the schools are very simple, with few books or supplies. In village primary

Most Cambodian children start school at age six.

schools, the buildings are simply wooden frames without windows. Children sit on hard wooden benches in front of long tables. In some schools, several children must share a book at the same time. Pens and paper are scarce. In other schools, each child has a paper workbook with pictures and problems.

In the floating village of Chong Khnoas on the Tonle Sap, the school is built on a bamboo raft. Children row canoes to school each day. They carry their books and lunch in a backpack. When a large boat passes by, the children inside the school sway from the wake.

Children must take boats to get to this floating school on the Tonle Sap.

Girls learn classical Cambodian dance at the School of Fine Arts in Phnom Penh.

Other Schools

Some talented children attend the School of Fine Arts in Phnom Penh. At this school, they study art, music, and dance. At temple schools, children learn Buddhist scriptures and Pali, the ancient religious language of Buddhism.

If students finish secondary school, they may go on to college. Cambodia's largest college is the Royal University of Phnom Penh. Students there study science and social science. Other institutions teach business, medicine, and technical subjects.

In the past, most well-educated Cambodians spoke French as a second language. Today, English has become more common than French.

In Cambodia, women take care of most of the household chores, such as washing dishes.

Women and Children

When a woman gets married in Cambodia, she does not take her husband's last name. Instead, she keeps her own name. In Cambodia, a woman has a very active role in the home. She is responsible for raising the children and taking care of the home. Many women also are in charge of the family budget.

Even though the mother does not take the father's last name, the children do. The Cambodian name is written and spoken by using the family name first and then the given name, or "first" name.

For many years, Cambodians did not keep track of their birthday. They only knew the animal year that they were born into, such as the year of the monkey or the year of the horse. Today, many Cambodians keep track of the actual day they were born.

By the age of four, Cambodian children are expected to feed and clothe themselves. Once they turn five, they may have to take care of a younger brother or sister. By the age of ten, boys must look after the family's livestock, and girls are supposed to help with household chores.

Many Cambodian children drop out of primary school because they need to work and help support their family. Some of these children work as street vendors or tour guides. Girls work as maids or help out in small restaurants. Some children work from 7:00 A.M. to 5:30 P.M. in fish processing plants or at

Many Cambodian children work at fishing or other jobs to help support their families.

Khmer Numbers

Muy	one
Pii	two
Bei	three
Buan	four
Bram	five
Bram muy	six
Bram pii	seven
Bram bei	eight
Bram buan	nine
Dawp	ten

cement factories. Young boys may find themselves behind the steering wheel of a commercial boat on the Tonle Sap.

Cambodian children do not have many toys. Even so, they still have fun by jumping into the cool waters of the Mekong or Tonle Sap or by playing a game of soccer in an empty city lot.

Respecting Elders

In Cambodia, ethnic background, age, education, talents, and wealth determine a person's social position. Respect for one's elders and superiors is part of the Cambodian culture. The older a person is, the higher his or her status becomes. Children are taught from a very young age to show respect for their elders.

Older people in Cambodia are shown great respect.

The Khmer alphabet is full of curves.

The Khmer Language

The official language of Cambodia is Khmer. Khmer has its own alphabet, which is full of beautiful curved letters. The language was influenced by the ancient Indian languages of Sanskrit and Pali. Though its roots go back thousands of years, words have continued to be added to Khmer from the Thai, Chinese, and French languages.

The Khmer language has twenty-four vowel sounds and thirty-three consonants. It is a poetic, musical language. In Khmer, words don't change to show past or present or plurals as they do in European languages. But the language does change depending on the status of the person you're talking to. For instance, special sets of words are used when talking to royalty and monks.

Common Khmer Words and Phrases

Johm riab sua	Hello
Kh' nyohm ch' muah	My name is . . .
Aw khohn	Thank you
Baat	Yes
Te	No
Arun suor sdei	Good morning
Sa-yoanh suor sdei	Good evening
Sohm toh	Excuse me

A Buddhist Nation

Buddhism is at the center of Cambodian life. Today, about 95 percent of Cambodians are Buddhist. But this was not always the case. The dominant religion in ancient Cambodia was Hinduism. Many buildings at Angkor were dedicated to Shiva, the Hindu god of creativity and destruction, and Vishnu, the preserver. By the beginning of the eleventh century, Buddhism was introduced into Cambodia. For a time, both Hinduism and Buddhism were popular religions. But by the fourteenth century, Buddhism had become the nation's dominant religion.

Opposite: **A Buddhist temple in Phnom Penh**

Giant Buddhist figures loom over Angkor Thom.

A Buddhist Nation **91**

Buddhism has about 350 million followers around the world. It is a particularly popular religion in Asia. Buddhism follows the teachings of an Indian prince named Siddhartha Gautama, who came to be called Buddha.

Siddhartha Gautama was born in the sixth century B.C. in Nepal, a country in the Himalayas between India and Tibet. He was born to rich parents and grew up surrounded by wealth. As he grew older, however, he became aware that the world was filled with suffering and unhappiness. Determined to change mankind's lot, he left his wife and baby son and became a wandering monk in search of religious knowledge.

After many years of traveling in northeastern India, he felt he had sorted out why mankind's life was so filled with

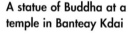

A statue of Buddha at a temple in Banteay Kdai

misery. When others heard what he had to say, they called him Buddha, meaning "enlightened one."

Buddha preached that life was a pattern of death and rebirth called reincarnation. A person's position in life depended on how he or she behaved in a previous life. For example, if a person did good deeds in a previous life, he would be happy and wealthy in his next life. But if a person did bad deeds in a previous life, his next life would be full of misery and sadness.

Buddha preached that as long as souls stay in the cycle of birth, death, and rebirth, they can never be completely free of misery and pain. The only way to break this cycle is to get rid of any attachment to worldly pleasures and follow the Middle Way and the Noble Eightfold Path.

The Middle Way is a way of conducting oneself in life. It includes not indulging too much in worldly desires but also not denying yourself too much. Rather, one should live life in the middle.

The Noble Eightfold Path is comprised of eight rules: (1) Make goals that include others, such as peace. (2) Do not do bad deeds such as killing, lying, stealing, and getting drunk; instead, perform good deeds. (3) Say nothing to harm others, and speak the truth. (4) Only participate in a job that will not harm others. (5) Resist evil; always try to do the right thing. (6) Be mentally alert and don't act thoughtlessly. (7) Practice meditation by thinking about the truth. (8) Control your feelings and thoughts.

Buddha died at the age of eighty. At that time, Buddhism was being formed as a religion.

Earning Merit

Buddhism is a religion based on doing good acts to earn merit. Performing good acts increases a person's good karma. Karma is everything a person does in one lifetime that may influence his or her fate in this life and the next.

Men earn merit by spending time in a monastery as a monk. Mothers earn merit when their sons become monks. Monks are important in Cambodian society. They are usually present at major ceremonies or events. People also earn merit by visiting shrines, feeding monks, and celebrating holy days.

Buddhism in Cambodia

Buddhism is divided into two main groups, Mahayana and Theravada, which follow different teachings and beliefs. In Cambodia, Mahayana Buddhism was practiced in the twelfth century during the reign of Jayavarman VII. But today, virtually all Cambodians belong to the Theravada school of Buddhism. *Theravada* means "way of the elders." It has been practiced in Cambodia since the fourteenth century.

A young monk holds incense.

The Lotus Flower

The lotus flower is the symbol of Buddha. A story says that when Buddha was born, his footprints became lotus flowers. Even today, the lotus flower is considered holy. Lotus flowers are often sold at temples to be given as an offering to the Buddha statue. Hundreds of lotus flowers are sculpted in stone at the Angkor ruins.

The lotus flower is a large flower that grows in freshwater wetlands. The young buds emerge out of the muddy water looking like hands folded in prayer. At the end of the long stem, a huge white and pink flower blooms. Its almond-shaped petals form a shallow bowl around a seedpod. White seeds cling to the seedpod's yellow center.

The Khmers use all parts of the lotus plant. They use it as food. Fibers from the stems are woven into fabric. The flowers are also part of their religion.

Theravada Buddhists stress that Buddha was an important historical figure and not a god. They also believe that only through lengthy meditation can a person achieve enlightenment. Those who achieve enlightenment pass straight to nirvana at death. Nirvana is a state where the spirit no longer desires to continue the cycle of reincarnation. Instead, the soul becomes released from all physical desires and maintains a state of eternal happiness.

Most Cambodian villages have temples with statues of Buddha. Temples also include a hall where classes and ceremonies are held, a kitchen, a pond, and a place for monks and nuns to live.

Buddhist nuns shave their heads.

Monks play a large role in Cambodian society. They spend much of their time meditating. They also take part in weddings, funerals, and other ceremonies. Monks wear orange or yellow robes. This makes them very easy to spot.

In 1975, about sixty-four thousand monks lived in Cambodia. But then the Khmer Rouge abolished all religion. Many temples were demolished. Many monks were killed. Others were forced to disrobe. Since the Khmer Rouge left power, Buddhism and monkhood have again become popular. At any given time, Cambodia is home to about sixty thousand practicing monks.

Women who have decided to live in the temple and study Buddha's teachings are called lay nuns. They dress in white and shave their heads. Lay nuns do not have as many rules to follow as monks. Because of this, they do not have the status in society that the monks have.

Life as a Monk

Many boys choose to become monks between the ages of thirteen and fifteen. Most boys are monks for less than a year. Very few Cambodians become monks for life. Men must be at least twenty-one years old before committing to become a monk for life.

Monks wear orange or yellow robes at all times. They must also follow ten precepts, or rules of conduct. These include telling the truth, not drinking alcohol, not singing or dancing, not sleeping on a raised bed, and not handling money. In addition, monks must also adhere to 227 other rules. They lead very simple lives, which are completely devoted to Buddhism and the temple.

Monks rise early in the morning for meditation and prayer. Meditation is the time when monks concentrate on the goal of stopping all desire. After meditation, the monks walk through neighborhoods begging for food. Monks cannot eat after noon. They fast for the rest of the day.

The Spirit World

Though Buddhism is the main religion of Cambodia, other beliefs are also important. Many Cambodians believe in spirits such as ghost, demons, animal spirits, and ancestral spirits. They believe that spirits can live anywhere, including in objects such as rocks, rivers, and trees. This belief in spirits often combines with Buddhism.

Many villagers keep a statue of Buddha inside their homes. Some villages also have spirit houses, where spirits supposedly live. Villagers leave food, flowers, and other items in front of the spirit house. They believe that if the spirit is not shown respect, it will cause mischief or bad fortune.

A shrine in Phnom Penh

About 3.5 percent of Cambodians are Muslim.

Some Cambodians wear special charms to protect them from evil. They also believe in fortune-tellers and astrologers. They may consult a fortune-teller when making important decisions.

Other Religions

Even though Buddhism is the most popular religion in Cambodia, some Cambodians practice other religions. The Cham are Muslims, followers of the religion of Islam. Muslims believe that there is only one God, who is called Allah. Muslims pray five times a day. In Cham communities, many women—like many Muslim women around the world—wear veils to cover their heads.

Several thousand Vietnamese in Cambodia are Roman Catholic. Some Christian organizations are also active in Cambodia. They help people in need and spread the teachings of Christianity. But so far, Christians have not had much success in converting the Cambodians.

Ancient Traditions

Cambodian ballet emphasizes good posture and slow movements.

Some of Cambodia's art forms go back a thousand years. Though the Khmer Rouge almost completely wiped out many of these arts, these beautiful traditions are making a strong comeback in modern Cambodia.

Dance

Cambodian dance is a source of intense national pride. Classical Cambodian ballet is filled with slow, graceful movements. This type of dancing relies heavily on the posture of the body and the movement of the hands. Different movements have different meanings. For example, crossing the arms over the chest means "very happy." If a hand is down, it means "alive."

Opposite: **Young girls learn a traditional Cambodian dance.**

Musicians accompany the dancers. They play drums, flutes, gongs, stringed instruments, and xylophones.

Cambodian ballet was developed during the Angkor Empire. Ancient dancers performed only before royalty. Their dances honored the gods. Ancient dancers started their training at a very early age, just as dancers do today. From the start, dancers are taught special exercises to loosen their joints and increase their flexibility. Some dancers are so flexible they can bend their fingers almost all the way back to their wrists.

Drums and xylophones are important in traditional Cambodian music.

Cambodian dancers wear elaborate costumes and jewelry.

Dancers' costumes are made out of beautiful embroidered silk. The dancers wear gold jewelry around necks, upper arms, wrists, and ankles. They also wear gold earrings and gold spiked crowns on their heads. Flowers sometimes decorate their hair. Traditionally, all the dancers in the royal ballet were women—even those dancing the male roles. Today, women still dance most of the roles. But men play the animal characters such as monkeys. Male dancers usually wear elaborate animal masks.

Many dances are based on ancient stories such as the Hindu epic called the "Ramayana." Some dances are based on folktales. These often include a clever monkey or hare.

The Royal Ballet was once part of the royal palace. This highly skilled dance troupe had about 200 members. The Khmer Rouge almost completely destroyed this dance troupe. By the time the Khmer Rouge lost power, only seventeen dancers survived. The Royal Ballet is slowly being revived by elderly teachers and government support.

Reviving Cambodia's Classical Dance

Chea Samy began studying classical dance when she was six years old. She trained to become a palace dancer for King Sisowath Monivong, the grandfather of King Norodom Sihanouk.

By the time she turned thirty, her expertise earned her a job as a dance teacher. But her career abruptly ended at age fifty-seven, when the Khmer Rouge took power. Instead of dressing in beautiful dance costumes, she wore the traditional black peasant outfit. Instead of dancing for kings, she was told to collect manure for fertilizer. When the Khmer Rouge asked her what her prior job had been, she told them that she was a street vendor because she feared being put to death.

Once the Khmer Rouge were forced from power, the Minister of Culture approached Chea Samy. He asked her to revive the nation's classical dance. With the help of a handful of musicians, she toured the country in search of suitable trainees. Chea Samy helped set up Phnom Penh's School of Fine Arts to train students in Cambodia's classical arts.

Young Cambodians learn traditional dance at the School of Fine Arts.

The School of Fine Arts

Phnom Penh's School of Fine Arts teaches traditional Khmer dances and crafts. Students have to audition to apply. Usually students start at the school when they are nine to twelve years old and continue until they are seventeen or eighteen.

Students at the school learn both folk dance—such as the magic scarf dance and the coconut dance—and classical dance, such as the ancient dances of Cambodia. Students also take classes in gymnastics and drama. In addition to the artistic classes, students must take the standard school curriculum such as math, reading, and writing.

Classical Literature

A famous story in classical Cambodian literature is called the "Reamker." This is the Cambodian version of the "Ramayana,"

Reap flies off through the sky after kidnapping Sita in this scene from the "Reamker."

an ancient Hindu story that has different versions in countries such as Laos, Indonesia, and Thailand. The Cambodian version contains some events from the original Indian version as well as events that have been changed to fit Theravada Buddhism.

The "Reamker" is about Prince Ream. He vanishes into the forest with his wife, Sita. While in the forest, another prince, Reap, sees Sita and falls in love with her. Prince Reap kidnaps Sita and takes her to his palace in Langka.

Prince Ream vows to rescue his wife. He asks for help from the Prince of the Monkeys. Together they attack Prince Reap at Langka. Prince Ream is victorious. He rescues Sita and is crowned king.

Cambodian Folktales

Legends and folktales are an important part of Cambodian culture. They are passed down from one generation to the next. One legend, called "Preah Ko Preah Keo," is about a cow named Preah Ko and a boy named Preah Keo who were born from one woman. The cow turns out to be magical and repeatedly saves the boy's life. The king of Siam finds out about Preah Ko's magical abilities and captures the cow and the boy. He takes them away, and they never return to Cambodia.

"The Clever Little Hare" is another traditional Khmer folktale. It is about a hare that gets stuck to the sap on the bottom of a tree stump. To get off the stump, the hare starts an argument with an approaching elephant. In its rage, the elephant picks the hare up off the stump. The hare convinces the elephant to throw him in a bush. This allows the hare to escape.

Cambodian Death Customs

Cambodians believe in reincarnation. When someone dies, ceremonies are held to honor that person and to send him or her on to the next life.

If a person dies in an accident or is murdered, the body is kept at the temple. These sorts of death are considered bad luck. If a person dies of natural causes, the body is kept at home. The body is washed, dressed, and placed in a coffin.

The body is then taken by car or is carried to the temple. A funeral party of monks and relatives accompany the body. Some family members may shave their heads to pay respect.

At the temple, the family and monks pray while walking three times around the crematorium, where the body will be burned. Most temples have crematoriums, but if they don't, a wooden structure is built to serve as one.

After the body is burned, the ashes are placed in an urn. Seven days after the person's death, another celebration is held in the home. Monks attend and pray to give the deceased a rebirth or reincarnation. One hundred days later, a smaller ceremony is held to remember the dead person.

Five towers rise above
Angkor Wat.

Architecture

Cambodia's ancient Angkor temples are one of the artistic and architectural wonders of the world. One of the main temples, Angkor Wat, is the largest religious building on the planet.

Visiting the temples is like stepping into a mysterious, magical world. A sandstone causeway or bridge leads to the main entrance of Angkor Wat. The causeway is lined with a stone railing that starts with a *naga*, a multiheaded snake. Horses graze in the green fields next to one of Angkor Wat's six libraries, while hundreds of dragonflies dart back and forth in the air. In the background, cicadas hum and birds sing, while steam rises off the hot jungle. And above it all, Angkor Wat's spirals point to the sky.

The temple area is enclosed by a huge moat more than 3 miles (5 km) around. Lotus and other water plants flourish in the water. Workers have to clean out the moat regularly. They spend four hours a day in the water pulling up water plants and rolling them up like carpets before dragging them to the shore.

Another temple, Ta Prohm, is partially covered in jungle. Gigantic banyan and kapok trees rise high into the sky. Their roots are woven into the ancient temple and have become part of it. Parrots squawk noisily as they fly above in the forest

Trees have taken over parts of Ta Prohm.

canopy. Inside the ruins is a building named The Way to Nirvana. In the alcove of this small stone structure, a visitor stands against the wall and pounds her chest. The sound echoes magically.

At many Angkor ruins, chickens scratch the ground and cows graze nearby. Peddlers follow visitors right up to the entrance of each temple. But inside, all is quiet except for the hushed tones of the visitors amazed by the craftsmanship of the ancient carvings and buildings.

The National Museum

The National Museum was built between 1917 and 1920. It consists of four galleries surrounding a courtyard with ponds filled with water lilies. The museum displays Cambodia's stone masterpieces. Visitors can view pottery and drums from ancient times. Other items on display are a carved boat cabin with intricate designs and a statue of eight-armed Vishnu that is more than 1,400 years old.

The museum also has a statue of Buddha that some visitors worship. People can buy incense to give to the statue. In front of the statue is a fortune book with a stick hanging from a string. To determine one's fortune, the book is placed on the person's head. The person then randomly puts the stick between two pages. The book is opened to that page, and the fortune is read in Khmer.

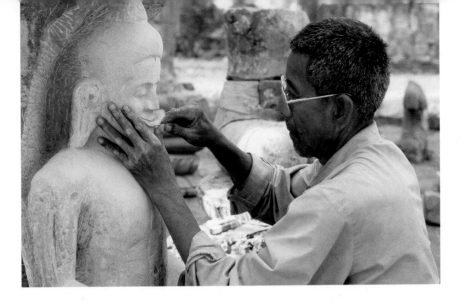

A sculptor carves an image of the Buddha out of stone.

Cambodian Handicrafts

Many different handicrafts are produced in Cambodia. Some artisans go to school in Phnom Penh to learn their skills, while others learn from other artisans living in their village. Some craftspeople make sculptures of wood and stone. Others use copper to form bowls, pots, and bells. Silver is pounded into bracelets, necklaces, and rings. Clay is molded into huge

Making Silk

Most silk thread in Cambodia is imported from Vietnam. But some Cambodians are starting to produce their own silk.

Silk is made by small creatures called silkworms. Silkworms that eat the leaves of mulberry trees produce the best quality of silk.

Silkworms form a soft cocoon about the size of a peanut. The outside of the cocoon has a stringy down layer, which is the silk. To remove the silk, the cocoon is submerged in hot water. This kills the silkworm. The silk is removed by pulling it off the cocoon as one long string.

Because a silk farm needs a constant supply of silk-worms, some of the cocoons are not boiled. Instead, the silkworms are allowed to emerge from their cocoon and become moths. The moths mate, and one female lays up to three hundred yellow eggs. After ten days, the eggs turn to gray. They are then moved to a wooden box with holes and covered with a wet cloth. In about two days, the eggs become silkworms. The worms are fed finely chopped mulberry leaves for six days. Over the next nine days, the worms are given big leaves, until they stop eating. Finally, the worms are moved to a branch or compartment so they can form a cocoon.

And the cycle starts again.

Boat races are the highlight of the annual Water Festival, which draws a million people.

jars to catch the monsoon rains. Leather is cut to make shadow puppets and pictures of Angkor Wat. Musical instruments are made from palm leaf, bamboo, and reeds. Cotton and silk are woven into kramas, shirts, and skirts.

Sports

Some Cambodian sports date back centuries. One of these ancient sports is boat racing. Cambodia's most famous boat races take place during the three-day Water Festival in November. Villagers hollow out logs that hold up to forty rowers. More than three hundred boat teams show up in Phnom Penh to take part in the races. The rowers wear brightly colored costumes, and the boats are painted in festive colors. People crowd the riverbanks to watch their village boat. Races are held for two days. The championship race takes place on the third day of the Water Festival.

More modern sports are played at Olympic Stadium in Phnom Penh. Volleyball, basketball, soccer, and swimming matches are held there.

Kickboxing is a popular sport in Cambodia. It is a type of freestyle fighting. Contestants are allowed to both kick and punch. Hundreds of people show up at kickboxing matches. Top local kickboxers are treated like celebrities in Cambodia.

Soccer games are often played at Olympic Stadium in Phnom Penh.

Quiet Villages, Noisy Streets

THE PACE OF DAY-TO-DAY LIFE IN CAMBODIA DIFFERS DEPENDing on where one lives. Urban life can be hectic and chaotic, whereas village life moves at a much slower pace.

Opposite: **Boys ride water buffalo in rural Cambodia.**

Village Life

Most Cambodians live in rural areas. Many live in farming villages of one hundred to four hundred people. Rural Cambodians build their own houses. Often, their neighbors help. The houses are made from bamboo, thatch, or wood.

Cambodians work together to build a neighbor's house.

The houses are built on stilts, which helps protect them from flooding. It also allows air to circulate and keeps out rodents and other pests. The extra space beneath the house is used as storage. Sometimes carts are parked there or clotheslines are strung to dry the laundry.

Very few Cambodian houses have gas or electric stoves. Instead, meals are cooked over a wood fire. In rural areas, cooking is done either in a separate house or outside in a fire pit covered with a thatched roof. Pots and pans hang from trees.

Rural houses in Cambodia have no toilet or running water. To take a bath, children dip a metal bowl into a large clay pot filled with warm water. Then they pour the water over themselves.

Many houses in Cambodia are built on stilts.

Uniquely Cambodian, the Krama

The krama is a piece of clothing unique to Cambodia. Kramas are like a scarf that is wrapped around the head. They are made from cotton or silk. Kramas often have a checkered pattern, usually blue and white or red and white. Every province in Cambodia has its own typical krama with unique colors.

Kramas are a useful part of daily life. They protect Cambodians from wind, sun, dust, and rain. Women carry babies, chickens, and small livestock in them.

They can quickly be turned into a cover for a bed or chair. Once folded, they become comfortable pillows.

Cambodians sleep on the floor on handmade sisal mats. Sisal is a strong natural fiber that is cool to sleep on. Pillows are made from the seeds of the kapok tree.

Rural Cambodians work long hours in the sun. They often wear a scarf called a *krama* to protect their heads and necks. They wrap a long piece of fabric called a sarong around their waist. Most either go barefoot or wear rubber sandals.

Life in a Floating Village

Some Cambodians who live near the Tonle Sap lake have an unusual life. Their whole world is on water. Houses float on bamboo. There are floating mechanic shops and restaurants. Sitting on a bamboo porch, one woman shaves another woman's head.

Inside floating houses, children and mothers swing on hammocks. Some houses even have televisions. Outside, chickens and pigs are kept in pens. Cats and dogs carefully walk around the perimeter of their home. No electric wires

Houses teeter above the Tonle Sap.

run to the floating villages. Instead, batteries are used to run the TV and appliances.

Children take baths in the muddy waters of the lake. River taxis buzz by, filled with people. In front of the floating police department, policemen doze while swinging back and forth on a hammock. Peddlers float from house to house to sell food and wares.

How to Play Tres

One popular Cambodian game is called *tres*. To play tres, you need a handful of sticks and a ball or small fruit. Place ten or twelve sticks onto a flat surface. Throw a ball or small fruit into the air, and with the same hand pick up a stick and then catch the ball before it lands. If you miss a stick or the ball, you lose your turn.

Pets

Pets are common in Cambodian villages. Many people keep dogs and cats. Cambodians are not as attached to their pets as westerners. Most people have pets because they are helpful around the house. Dogs warn when strangers are approaching. Cats catch mice. Pets that do not do their duty are of no use to the family. Pets are often named after their fur color, such as brown, white, or black. If a pet works hard and pleases its owner, it may be named after a flower. Cambodians do not mourn when their pet dies. Instead, they get a new pet.

Cows and water buffaloes are extremely important to Cambodian families. They are essential for farming. These animals are treated with much respect and are even thought of as members of the family.

Children get a ride through a flooded rice field.

Cities such as Phnom Penh are much noisier than villages. The streets are filled with cars and scooters. Colorful billboards balance against tall buildings. Because of the many years of French control, Phnom Penh has wide avenues and many old western-style buildings.

Motorcycles whiz by the colorful Central Market.

One of these old buildings is the Central Market. It was built between 1935 and 1937 in the sleek art deco style of the time. Almost anything can be found at the Central Market. Walking the narrow aisles, shoppers can choose among snails, clothes, woodcarvings, toilet paper, fruit, books, jewelry, pork feet, and chunky red meat hanging on hooks in the sweltering heat.

Shoppers can buy practically anything at Phnom Penh's Central Market.

Guests at a Cambodian wedding enjoy a special feast of pigs' heads.

Food

The staples of the Cambodian diet are rice and fish. Cambodians only eat chicken, beef, or pork on special occasions. Dessert is also served only on special days. It is made with coconut milk and sugar.

Fish is especially abundant during November. This is the month that the flow of the Tonle Sap River reverses. Cambodians build dams to catch the fish as they flow back toward the lake. They trap huge schools of fish. The fish are quickly pulled out of the water. Some are dried and salted. Fresh fish is usually grilled and may be served in small chunks wrapped in spinach or lettuce leaves.

Cambodians eat with chopsticks, spoons, or fingers. An elaborate meal may have many plates for the different dishes served. In a rural home, however, the family often eats out of the same platter.

Common Foods in Khmer

tai	tea
teuk	water
t'ray	fish
saich	meat
num pung	bread
moan	chicken

Poat Dot (Cambodian Grilled Corn)

Ingredients:

3 ears of corn, husks removed

Vegetable oil, for brushing

1 tablespoon fish sauce

1 tablespoon water

2 teaspoons sugar

$\frac{1}{2}$ teaspoon salt

1 green onion, sliced thin

Directions:

Place an ungreased cast-iron skillet over medium heat. Lightly brush the corn with vegetable oil and put it in the skillet. Cook for about 15 minutes, turning the corn over every 2 to 3 minutes.

In a bowl, stir together the fish sauce, water, sugar, and salt until dissolved. Heat the mixture in a saucepan until very hot. Add green onions and cook for about 1 minute. Remove the saucepan from the stove and cool. Then brush the sauce all over the cooked corn, and eat.

Poor Cambodian farmers usually have only two meals a day. More successful farmers will eat three. They may begin their day with a snack such as a piece of fruit. The first large meal is at around 9 or 10 A.M. The next large meal is around noon, and the last one is at about 5:00 P.M.

Rice with soup is served at most meals. Fish and vegetables are also served. Tea is drunk during meals and throughout the day.

Rice is a staple of the Cambodian diet.

Unusual Cambodian Foods

Pong Tea Kon	A special duck egg that has a baby duck in it ready to hatch.
Fried Spiders	These spiders are bred in holes in the ground and then are caught and fried. Fried spiders can be bought at the Central Market in Phnom Penh and elsewhere.
Durian	A fruit with a strong, horrible odor, similar to smelly socks. Durians have a creamy, sweet center.
Locusts	These large insects, which look like grasshoppers, are fried and served as a crunchy snack.

Cambodians often flavor their food with ginger, mint, lemongrass, sugar, and peppers. Dishes in Cambodia have been influenced by China, India, and Europe. Cambodian food is similar to Thai food, except it is not as spicy and it has more sauce.

A woman sells fried spiders.

Being Cambodian

The Buddhist religion affects how Cambodians interact with each other. Cambodians never sit with the soles of their feet facing a Buddha image or any other person. Also, in Buddhism, a person's head is the most sacred part of the body. It is considered rude and inappropriate to touch another person's head,

A young girl gives the traditional Cambodian greeting.

even a child's. Showing anger or raising one's voice is thought to bring shame on oneself. A Cambodian who encounters an angry person will ignore that person and be embarrassed for him or her.

Cambodians greet each other by placing their hands in a prayer position in front of their chest without touching their body. They then give a slight bow. It is considered disrespectful to not return a greeting.

The Khmer Lunar Calendar

The Khmer calendar is based on the cycle of the moon, or the lunar cycle. The date of some celebrations varies from year to year because the lunar cycle does not match up with the twelve months used in western calendars.

National Festivals and Holidays in Cambodia

Victory Day—celebrates the fall of the Khmer Rouge in 1979	January 7
International Women's Day	March 8
Khmer New Year	Mid-April
Buddha's Birthday	April or May
Labor Day	May 1
Royal Ploughing Ceremony	May 17
The Feast of the Ancestors	September or October
King Norodom Sihanouk's Birthday	October 30–31
The Water Festival	October or November
Independence Day from France	November 9

Cambodians have lived through many years of war and conflict. And through it all, they have maintained their ancient and sacred customs. Many people want to forget the old hostilities. But no one wants to forget the polite rules and age-old habits that make them Cambodian.

Young Cambodians show off their proud traditions.

Timeline

Cambodian History

Humans begin to occupy Laang Spean cave in what is now northwestern Cambodia.	7000 B.C.
Cambodians domesticate animals and start growing rice.	2000 B.C.
Indian culture begins to seep into Cambodia.	100 B.C.
The kingdom of Funan begins in Cambodia.	A.D. 300
The kingdom of Zhen-la is established. Buddhism is introduced to Cambodia.	550
Jayavarman II comes into power and founds the Angkorean Empire.	802
King Suryavarman II begins construction on Angkor Wat.	1130
Chams pillage the Angkor temple.	1177
King Jayavarman VII drives the Chams out and builds a city called Angkor Thom.	1181
The kingdom of Siam captures Angkor Thom.	1431
Vietnam and Siam vie for control of Cambodia.	1700s–1800s

World History

2500 B.C.	Egyptians build the Pyramids and the Sphinx in Giza.
563 B.C.	The Buddha is born in India.
A.D. 313	The Roman emperor Constantine recognizes Christianity.
610	The Prophet Muhammad begins preaching a new religion called Islam.
1054	The Eastern (Orthodox) and Western (Roman) Churches break apart.
1066	William the Conqueror defeats the English in the Battle of Hastings.
1095	Pope Urban II proclaims the First Crusade.
1215	King John seals the Magna Carta.
1300s	The Renaissance begins in Italy.
1347	The Black Death sweeps through Europe.
1453	Ottoman Turks capture Constantinople, conquering the Byzantine Empire.
1492	Columbus arrives in North America.
1500s	The Reformation leads to the birth of Protestantism.
1776	The Declaration of Independence is signed.
1789	The French Revolution begins.

Cambodian History

King Norodom signs the Protectorate Treaty with France.	1863
The French force King Norodom to accept French control of Cambodia.	1887
The French choose eighteen-year-old Norodom Sihanouk to be the Cambodian king.	1941
Cambodia regains its independence from France.	1953
Lon Nol overthrows King Norodom Sihanouk and renames the country the Khmer Republic.	1970
The Khmer Rouge overthrow the Lon Nol government.	1975
Between one million and two million Cambodians die at the hands of the Khmer Rouge.	1975–1979
The Vietnamese battle the Khmer Rouge and capture Phnom Penh. The new government is called the People's Republic of Kampuchea.	1979
The Vietnamese withdraw from Cambodia.	1989
Warring factions in Cambodia sign a peace plan.	1991
Cambodia holds its first elections in twenty years.	1993
The last Khmer Rouge leaders surrender.	1998
King Norodom Sihanouk quits the throne due to poor health. His son, King Norodom Sihamoni, succeeds him.	2004

World History

1865	The American Civil War ends.
1914	World War I breaks out.
1917	The Bolshevik Revolution brings communism to Russia.
1929	Worldwide economic depression begins.
1939	World War II begins, following the German invasion of Poland.
1945	World War II ends.
1957	The Vietnam War starts.
1969	Humans land on the moon.
1975	The Vietnam War ends.
1979	Soviet Union invades Afghanistan.
1983	Drought and famine in Africa.
1989	The Berlin Wall is torn down, as communism crumbles in Eastern Europe.
1991	Soviet Union breaks into separate states.
1992	Bill Clinton is elected U.S. president.
2000	George W. Bush is elected U.S. president.
2001	Terrorists attack World Trade Towers, New York and the Pentagon, Washington, D.C.

Fast Facts

Official name: The Kingdom of Cambodia

Capital: Phnom Penh

Official language: Khmer

The Old French Quarter in
Siem Reap

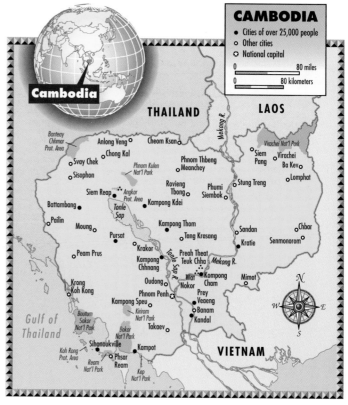

Cambodia's flag

Siem Reap Province

Official religion:	Theravada Buddhism
Year of founding:	1953
Founder:	King Norodom Sihanouk
National anthem:	"Nokoreach" ("Royal Kingdom")
Government:	Constitutional monarchy
Chief of state:	King
Area:	69,898 square miles (181,035 sq km)
Greatest distance east to west:	350 miles (563 km)
Greatest distance north to south:	280 miles (451 km)
Latitude and longitude of geographic center:	13° N, 105° E
Bordering countries:	Thailand to the north and northwest, Laos to the north, Vietnam to the east and southeast
Highest elevation:	Phnum Aoral, 5,948 ft. (1,813 m)
Lowest elevation:	Sea level along the Gulf of Thailand
Average temperature:	78°F (25.6°C) in January; 85°F (29.5°C) in April
National population:	13,363,421 (July 2004)

Banteay Srei temple

Cambodian riels

Population of largest provinces (1998):

Kompong Cham	1,608,914
Kandal	1,075,125
Prey Veaeng	946,042
Battambang	793,129
Takaev	790,168
Siem Reap	696,164

Famous landmarks:

- ▶ *Angkor Wat*, Siem Reap
- ▶ *Angkor Thom*, Siem Reap
- ▶ *Tuol Sleng Genocide Museum*, Phnom Penh
- ▶ *Killing Fields Memorial*, outside Phnom Penh
- ▶ *National Museum*, Phnom Penh
- ▶ *Wat Phnom*, Phnom Penh
- ▶ *Independence Monument*, Phnom Penh
- ▶ *Royal Palace*, Phnom Penh
- ▶ *Silver Pagoda*, Phnom Penh

Industry: Cambodia's economy is based on agriculture, mainly rice and fishing. Recently, the garment industry has expanded, and clothes are now a major export.

Currency: The Cambodian riel. In February 2005, US$1 equaled 4,002 Cambodian riel.

System of weights and measures: Metric system

Literacy rate (1998): 80.8% (men)
59.3% (women)

Cambodian schoolchildren

King Norodom Sihanouk

Common words and phrases:

Johm nab sua	Hello
Kh' nyohm ch' muah	My name is . . .
Aw khohn	Thank you
Baat (for men)	Yes
Jaa (for women)	Yes
Te	No
Arun suor sdei	Good morning
Sa-yoanh suor sdei	Good evening
Sohm toh	Excuse me

Famous Cambodians:

King Jayavarman II (ca. 770–850)
First ruler of the Angkor kingdom

King Jayavarman VII (ca. 1120–1250)
Drove the Chams out of Cambodia and expanded the Angkor kingdom

King Norodom Sihanouk (1922–)
Helped Cambodia achieve independence from France. Reigned 1941–1955 and 1993–2004.

Pol Pot (1925–1998)
Leader of the Khmer Rouge

King Suryavarman II (?–1150)
Built Angkor Wat

To Find Out More

Books

- *Cambodia: A Portrait of the Country Through Its Festivals and Traditions.* Danbury, Conn.: Grolier, 1999.

- De Silva, Dayaneetha. *Cambodia.* Milwaukee: Garth Stevens Publishing, 2000.

- Dramer, Kim. *The Mekong River.* New York: Franklin Watts, 2001.

- Nobleman, Marc Tyler. *Cambodia.* Mankato, Minn.: Bridgestone, 2003.

- St. Pierre, Stephanie. *Teenage Refugees from Cambodia.* New York: Rosen, 1995.

- Sheehan, Sean. *Cambodia.* Tarrytown, N.Y.: Marshall Cavendish, 1996.

Videos

- *Asia Close-Up: Japan and Cambodia.* Maryknoll World Productions, 1996.

- *Emerging Burma and Cambodia.* Questar Video, 1995.

Web Sites

▶ **Embassy of Cambodia**
http://www.embassy.org/cambodia/
*On this Web site, you can play the
national anthem, read a biography of
King Sihanouk, and find many links.*

▶ **Go Cambodia**
http://www.gocambodia.com
*Information on Cambodia's history and
geography, Angkor temples, behavior
codes, Buddhism, and more.*

▶ **CIA Factbook**
http://www.cia.gov/cia/publications/
factbook/geos/cb.html
*Filled with facts about Cambodia's
people, government, and economy.*

Embassy

▶ **The Royal Cambodian Embassy**
4530 16th Street NW
Washington, D.C. 20011
(202) 726-7742

Index

Page numbers in *italics* indicate illustrations.

Meet the Author

S̲ARA L̲OUISE K̲RAS'S love for travel began when she was a little girl. Her mother took their family to many of the amazing national parks around the United States. Sara continued this tradition of travel as she got older. She has lived in Zimbabwe, South Africa, and England. In addition, she has explored Australia, Kenya, Thailand, Cambodia, the Maldives, Japan, Costa Rica, Mexico, Canada, Denmark, and France.

While visiting Cambodia, Sara was able to talk to government officials about their country. She also spent a great deal of time visiting the ruins in the Angkor area. Sara was amazed at how polite and mannerly the Cambodians acted toward her during her visit.

"I have always been fascinated with other cultures and ways of life," says Sara. "Seeing people live a completely different lifestyle to what I am used to makes me appreciate what we have. It also helps me to realize that different ways of doing

things may be better than what I know. Finding out about these cultures and then telling children about them is one of my favorite things to do. I love to get children excited about the world they live in and to get them curious to find out more."

Sara grew up in Washington State, Texas, and Colorado. She has always loved the outdoors. She enjoys exploring nature and seeing animals in their natural habitat. She currently lives in Glendale, California, with her husband and cat. Sara is the author of more than a dozen books for children. This is her first book for Children's Press.

Photo Credits

Photographs © 2005:

akg-Images, London: 43 bottom
(François Guenet), 7 top, 108
Alamy Images/M. Joseph: 123
AP/Wide World Photos: 51 (APTN), 60
(Andy Eames), 59 (David Longstreath)
Asia Images Group/John McDermott:
24, 131 bottom
Bruce Coleman Inc.: 42, 116, 118 (John
Elk III), 30 bottom (Rod Williams)
China Span/Keren Su: 53, 131 top
Corbis Images: 54 (Bettmann), 87
(Pablo Corral Vega), 25, 30 top
(Michael Freeman), 37 (Japack
Company), 121 (Earl & Nazima
Kowall), 61 (Adrees Latif/Reuters),
22 (Joe McDonald), 11, 14, 15, 39,
72, 92, 106, 111, 113 (Kevin R.
Morris), 85, 86, 95 (Kevin R. Morris/
Bohemian Nomad Picturemakers),
77 (Richard T. Nowitz), 69 top (Tim
Page), 55, 133 bottom (Li Peng), 12
(Steve Raymer), cover, 6, 126 (Reza/
Webistan), 70 (Paul Seheult/Eye
Ubiquitous), 74, 99 (Chor Sokunthea/
Reuters), 107 (Sukree Sukplang/
Reuters), 40 (Luca I. Tettoni),
115 (Tom Wagner), 29 (Stuart
Westmorland), 6, 73, 94, 114, 119,
122, 124 (Michael S. Yamashita)
Corbis SABA/Tom Wagner: 50
Corbis Sygma/Thierry Orban: 47
Danita Delimont Stock Photography/
Jon Arnold: 89
Dave G. Houser/HouserStock, Inc.: 98

David Sanger Photography: 76
Getty Images/Chhoy Pisei/AFP: 57
Joe Kras: 13, 18, 48, 49, 52, 62, 71, 78,
80, 83, 84, 100, 101, 105, 109, 110,
112, 125, 132 bottom, 133 top
John Elk III: 75, 90
Lonely Planet Images: 104 (John
Banagan), 21 (Cheryl Conlon),
82 (Nick Ray)
Magnum Photos/John Vink: 19, 56, 65,
69 bottom
Mary Evans Picture Library: 43 top
Nature Picture Library Ltd./Nick
Barwick: 2
Network Aspen: 81 (Jeffrey Aaronson),
97 (Tibor Bognar)
Peter Arnold Inc./Gerard Soury: 34
Photo Researchers, NY: 9 (George
Holton), 35 (Tom McHugh/
Steinhart Aquarium), 33 (Merlin
D. Tuttle/Bat Conservation
International), 31 (Terry Whittaker)
Phototake/Newman & Associates: 28
Robert & Linda Mitchell: 36, 120
Robertstock.com/K. Rice: 127
Stone/Getty Images/Art Wolfe: 32
Tom Till Photography, Inc.: 23
TRIP Photo Library: 16 (A. Gasson),
91 (Patrick Syder)
Woodfin Camp & Associates: 7 bot-
tom, 26, 27, 38, 102, 103, 130 left
(David Henley/CPA), 8, 64, 88, 96,
117, 132 top (Mireille Vautier)
Maps by XNR Productions, Inc.